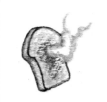

Everyday Machines

Amazing Devices We Take For Granted

John Kelly
David Burnie and Obin

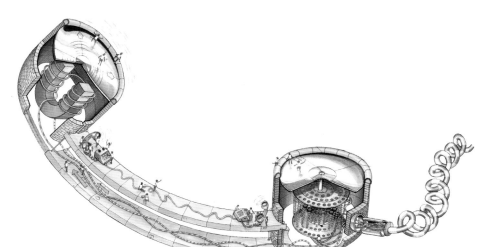

Turner Publishing, Inc.

ATLANTA

A Marshall Edition
Conceived, edited, and designed by Marshall Editions,
170 Piccadilly, London W1V 9DD

Library of Congress Cataloging-in-Publication Data
Burnie, David.
    Everyday machines: amazing devices we take for granted / David
Burnie; John Kelly and Obin [illustrators].
        p. cm.
    ISBN 1-57036-155-X
    1. Machinery–Juvenile literature. [1. Machinery.]   I. Kelly,
John, 1964–   ill.   II. Obin, ill.   III. Title
TJ147.B83   1995
621.8–dc20   95-11950
                                                          CIP
                                                          AC

First Published in the U.S.A. in 1995 by
Turner Publishing, Inc.
A Subsidiary of Turner Broadcasting System, Inc.
1050 Techwood Drive, N.W.
Atlanta, Georgia 30318

Distributed by Andrews and McMeel
A Universal Press Syndicate Company
4900 Main Street
Kansas City, Missouri 64112

First Edition 10 9 8 7 6 5 4 3 2 1

Project Editor: Kate Scarborough
Managing Editor: Kate Phelps
Managing Designer: Ralph Pitchford
Editorial Director: Cynthia O'Brien
Art Director: Branka Surla
Proof Reader: Isabella Raeburn
Production: Janice Storr and Angela Kew

Supervising Editor, Turner Publishing: Crawford Barnett
Copy Editor, Turner Publishing: Lauren Emerson

Originated by CLG, Verona, Italy
Printed and bound in Italy by
Officine Grafiche De Agostini—Novara

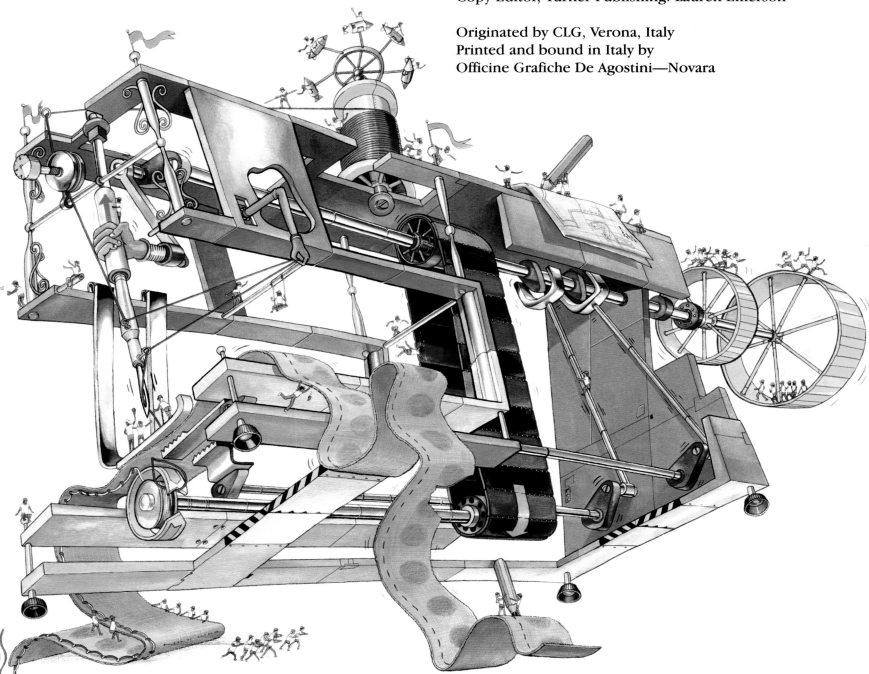

Contents

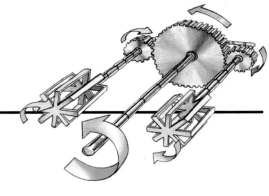

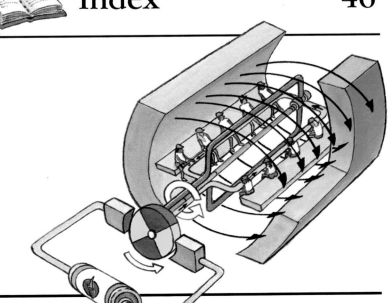

Introduction

Without machines, our lives would be very different. Simple jobs, such as washing clothes or cooking, would take much longer than they do now, and it would be impossible to telephone your friends or watch television.

Machines require energy to function. One method of producing energy is to burn fuel (see illustration below). Other methods include using the power of the sun (solar energy) and using the power of moving water (hydroelectric energy). Machines use this power by converting one form of energy into another. For example, some machines change the energy of movement into electrical energy, or electricity, while others change electricity into heat, light, or back into movement. Explore the power plant below to see how these processes work.

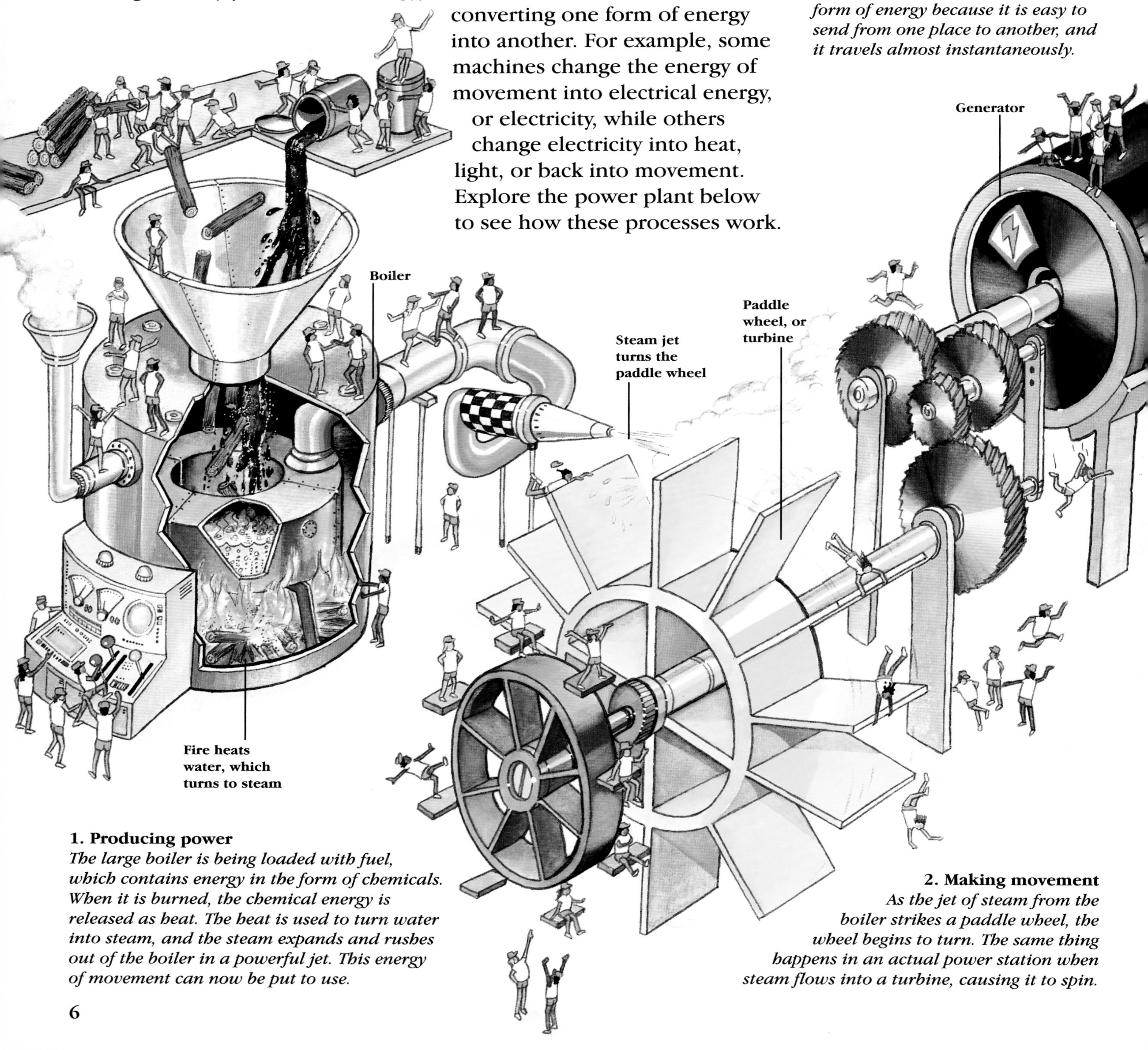

3. From movement to electricity
When the paddle wheel spins, a device called a generator turns the rotational energy into electrical energy. Electricity is a very useful form of energy because it is easy to send from one place to another, and it travels almost instantaneously.

Generator

Boiler

Paddle wheel, or turbine

Steam jet turns the paddle wheel

Fire heats water, which turns to steam

1. Producing power
The large boiler is being loaded with fuel, which contains energy in the form of chemicals. When it is burned, the chemical energy is released as heat. The heat is used to turn water into steam, and the steam expands and rushes out of the boiler in a powerful jet. This energy of movement can now be put to use.

2. Making movement
As the jet of steam from the boiler strikes a paddle wheel, the wheel begins to turn. The same thing happens in an actual power station when steam flows into a turbine, causing it to spin.

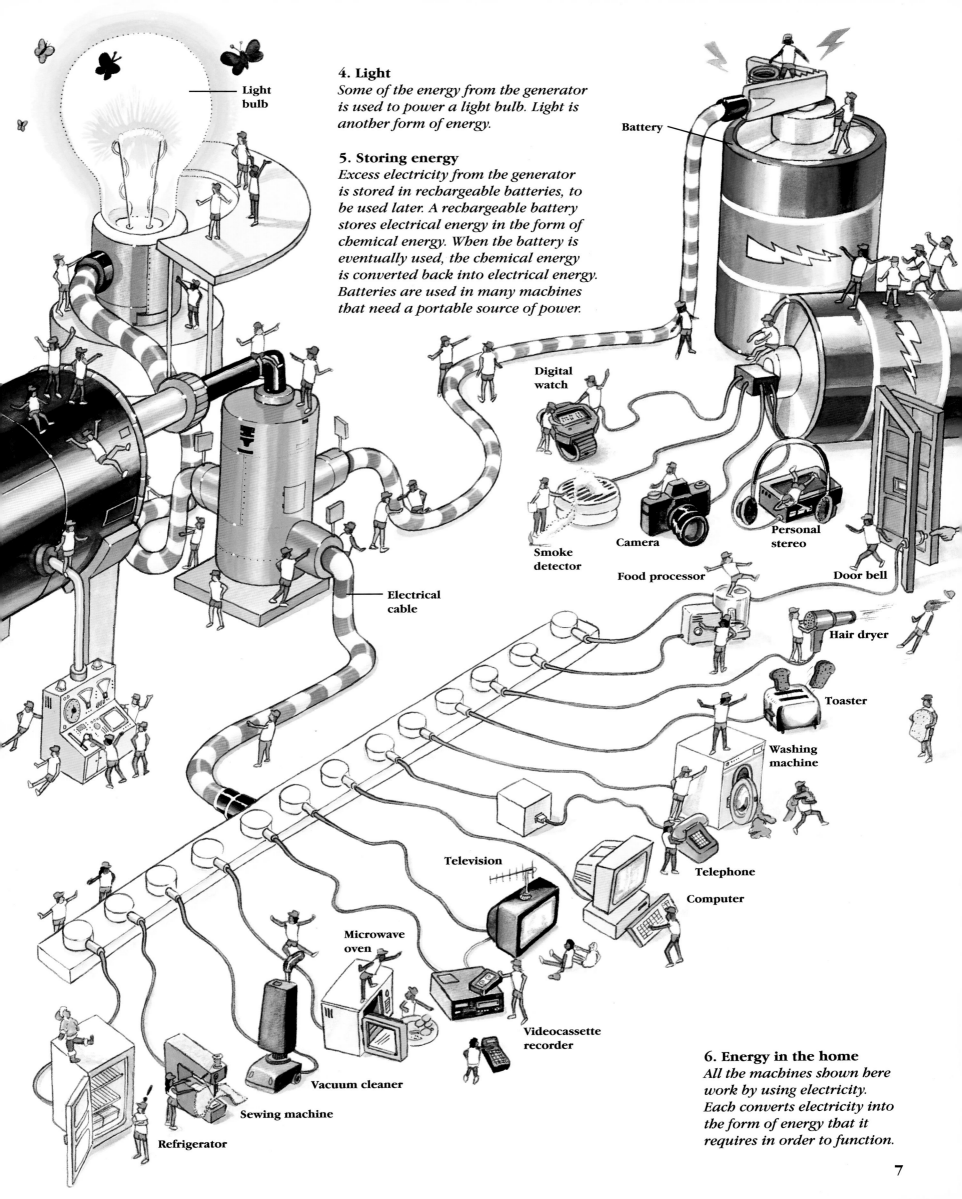

4. Light
Some of the energy from the generator is used to power a light bulb. Light is another form of energy.

Light bulb

5. Storing energy
Excess electricity from the generator is stored in rechargeable batteries, to be used later. A rechargeable battery stores electrical energy in the form of chemical energy. When the battery is eventually used, the chemical energy is converted back into electrical energy. Batteries are used in many machines that need a portable source of power.

Battery

Digital watch

Electrical cable

Smoke detector

Camera

Personal stereo

Food processor

Door bell

Hair dryer

Toaster

Washing machine

Telephone

Computer

Television

Microwave oven

Vacuum cleaner

Videocassette recorder

Refrigerator

Sewing machine

6. Energy in the home
All the machines shown here work by using electricity. Each converts electricity into the form of energy that it requires in order to function.

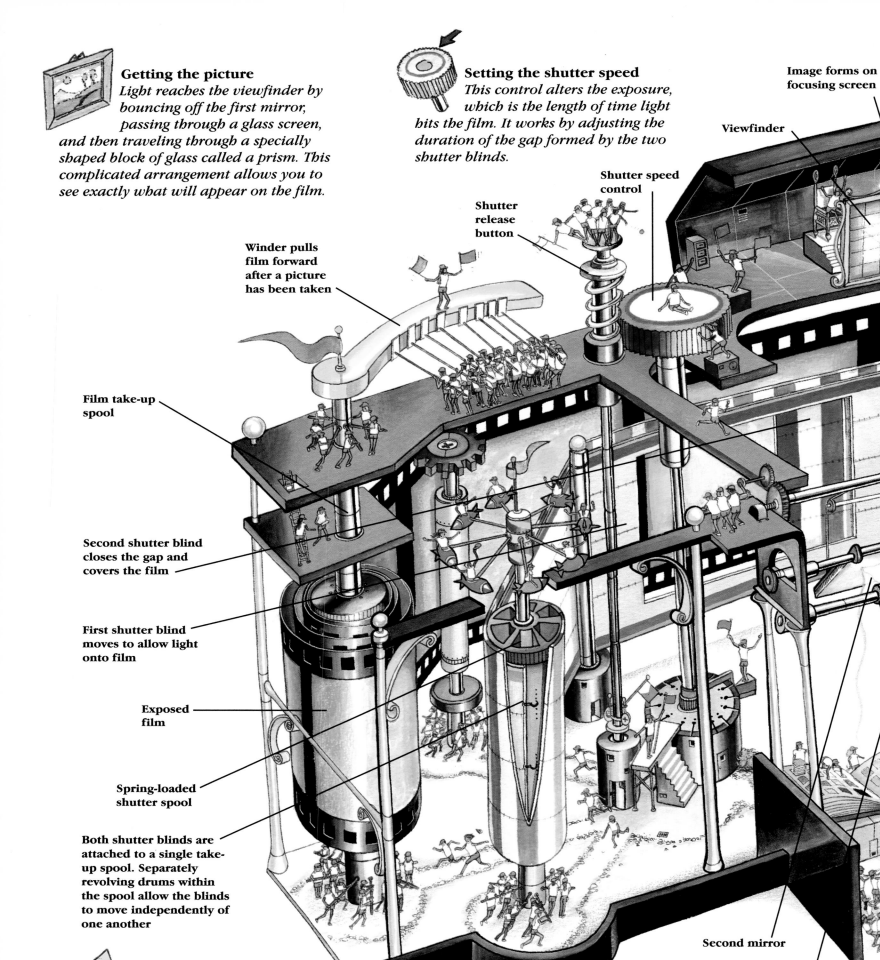

Getting the picture
Light reaches the viewfinder by bouncing off the first mirror, passing through a glass screen, and then traveling through a specially shaped block of glass called a prism. This complicated arrangement allows you to see exactly what will appear on the film.

Setting the shutter speed
This control alters the exposure, which is the length of time light hits the film. It works by adjusting the duration of the gap formed by the two shutter blinds.

Image forms on focusing screen

Viewfinder

Shutter speed control

Shutter release button

Winder pulls film forward after a picture has been taken

Film take-up spool

Second shutter blind closes the gap and covers the film

First shutter blind moves to allow light onto film

Exposed film

Spring-loaded shutter spool

Both shutter blinds are attached to a single take-up spool. Separately revolving drums within the spool allow the blinds to move independently of one another

Second mirror

First mirror

Aperture control

Two-way split
After passing through the lenses and the iris diaphragm, the light hits two mirrors. The first mirror sends most of the light upward to the focusing screen. The rest of the light hits the second mirror and is used to set the camera's aperture automatically. When you take a picture, both mirrors flip up and out of the way.

Open and shut
Before you take a picture, the film is covered by a shutter blind. When you press the shutter release, this shutter blind suddenly flicks past the film, and a gap lets light shine through it. A fraction of a second later, a second blind follows the first one, covering the film up again.

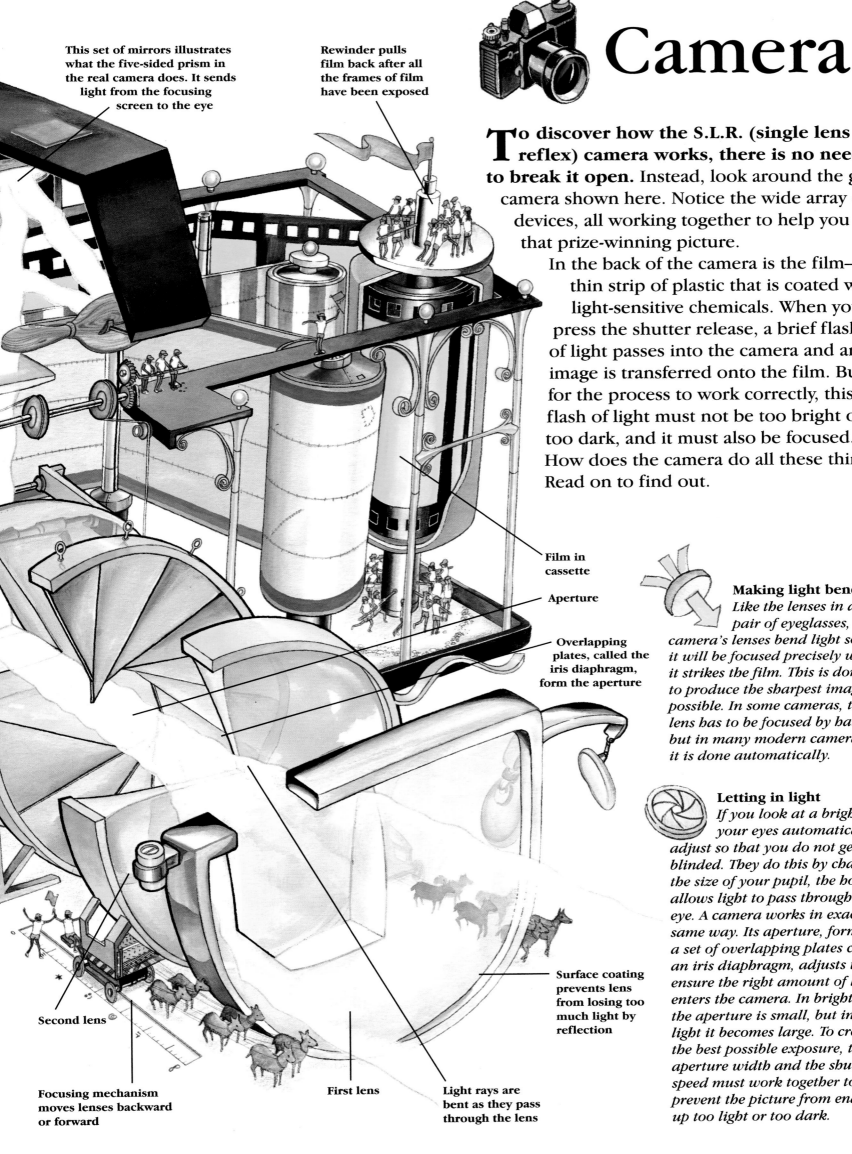

Camera

This set of mirrors illustrates what the five-sided prism in the real camera does. It sends light from the focusing screen to the eye

Rewinder pulls film back after all the frames of film have been exposed

To discover how the S.L.R. (single lens reflex) camera works, there is no need to break it open. Instead, look around the giant camera shown here. Notice the wide array of devices, all working together to help you take that prize-winning picture.

In the back of the camera is the film—a thin strip of plastic that is coated with light-sensitive chemicals. When you press the shutter release, a brief flash of light passes into the camera and an image is transferred onto the film. But for the process to work correctly, this flash of light must not be too bright or too dark, and it must also be focused. How does the camera do all these things? Read on to find out.

Film in cassette

Aperture

Overlapping plates, called the iris diaphragm, form the aperture

Making light bend
Like the lenses in a pair of eyeglasses, the camera's lenses bend light so that it will be focused precisely where it strikes the film. This is done to produce the sharpest image possible. In some cameras, the lens has to be focused by hand, but in many modern cameras, it is done automatically.

Letting in light
If you look at a bright light, your eyes automatically adjust so that you do not get blinded. They do this by changing the size of your pupil, the hole that allows light to pass through your eye. A camera works in exactly the same way. Its aperture, formed by a set of overlapping plates called an iris diaphragm, adjusts to ensure the right amount of light enters the camera. In bright light the aperture is small, but in dim light it becomes large. To create the best possible exposure, the aperture width and the shutter speed must work together to prevent the picture from ending up too light or too dark.

Surface coating prevents lens from losing too much light by reflection

Second lens

Focusing mechanism moves lenses backward or forward

First lens

Light rays are bent as they pass through the lens

Doorbell

If you have ever wondered how a doorbell works, here is your chance to find out. Like many machines, a doorbell uses electricity to operate. When a button is pressed, electricity is used to produce a magnetic field that will pull a hammer into a bell, making it ring. But a bell that rings only once would not attract much attention. Luckily, this doorbell is designed to keep clanging as long as the button is depressed. And the result is a noise that you simply cannot ignore.

ELECTRICITY AND A MAGNETIC FIELD

When electricity passes through a metal wire, a magnetic field forms around the wire. This can be seen by surrounding the wire with compasses. Normally they all point north. However, as soon as electricity flows, they show the field created around the wire. The wire now has the qualities of a magnet, and can attract and repel metal objects.

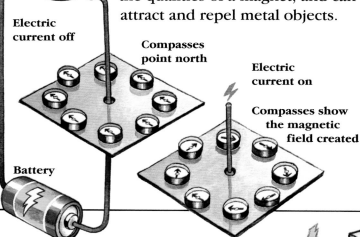

Switch

Electric current off

Battery

Compasses point north

Electric current on

Compasses show the magnetic field created

Switch operated by pressing bell button

Springs pulling movable contact back to complete circuit again

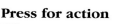

Press for action
When someone rings a doorbell, the effect is truly electric. The button completes a circuit, and electricity begins to flow. To find out what happens next, follow the wires around the page.

Temporary attraction
An ordinary magnet has a continuous pull, and would therefore not be of much use in a doorbell. An electromagnet is different because it only pulls when electricity is flowing. The current travels in coils around the U-shaped bar and produces a magnetic field. The field tugs at the hammer, and the bell rings. As soon as the current stops, the magnetic field vanishes and a spring pulls the hammer back.

Power transformer

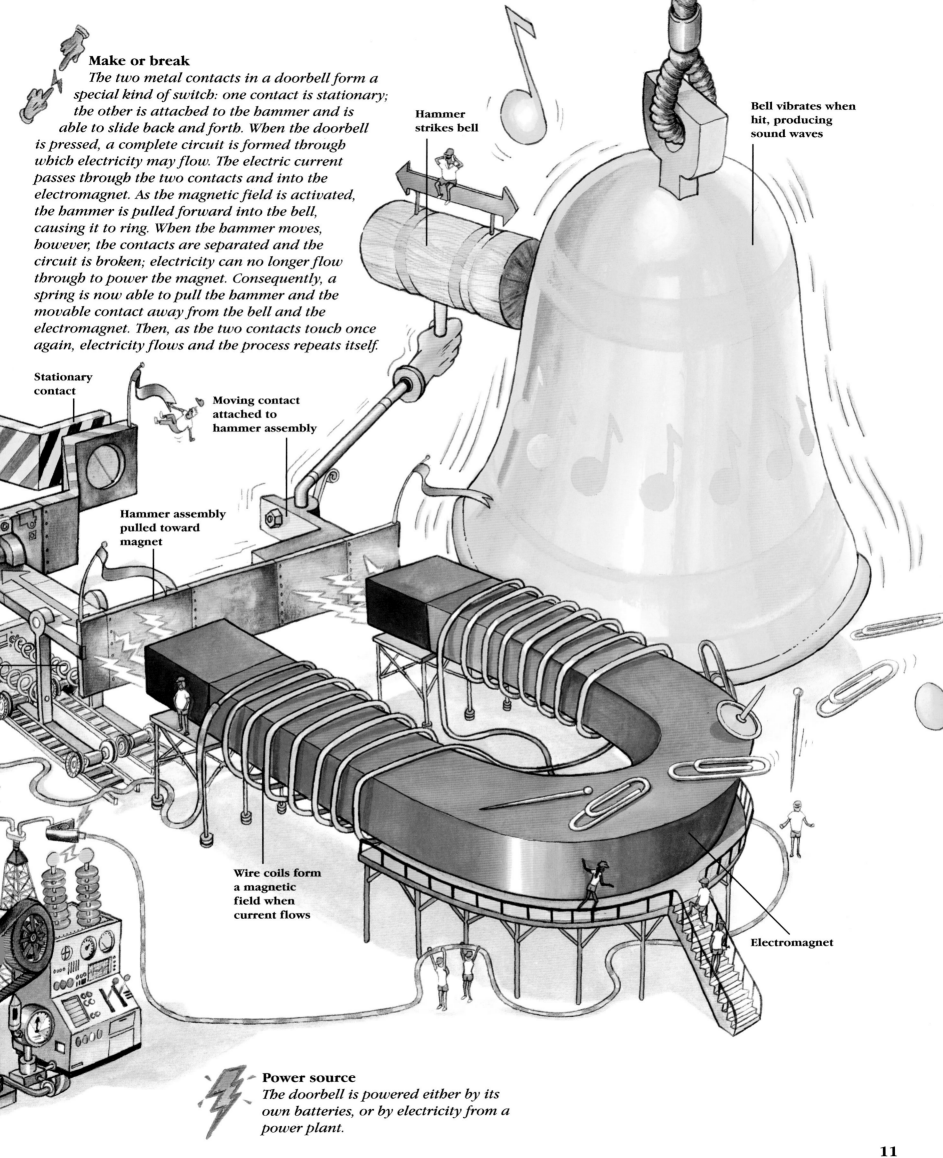

Make or break

The two metal contacts in a doorbell form a special kind of switch: one contact is stationary; the other is attached to the hammer and is able to slide back and forth. When the doorbell is pressed, a complete circuit is formed through which electricity may flow. The electric current passes through the two contacts and into the electromagnet. As the magnetic field is activated, the hammer is pulled forward into the bell, causing it to ring. When the hammer moves, however, the contacts are separated and the circuit is broken; electricity can no longer flow through to power the magnet. Consequently, a spring is now able to pull the hammer and the movable contact away from the bell and the electromagnet. Then, as the two contacts touch once again, electricity flows and the process repeats itself.

Hammer strikes bell

Bell vibrates when hit, producing sound waves

Stationary contact

Moving contact attached to hammer assembly

Hammer assembly pulled toward magnet

Wire coils form a magnetic field when current flows

Electromagnet

Power source

The doorbell is powered either by its own batteries, or by electricity from a power plant.

11

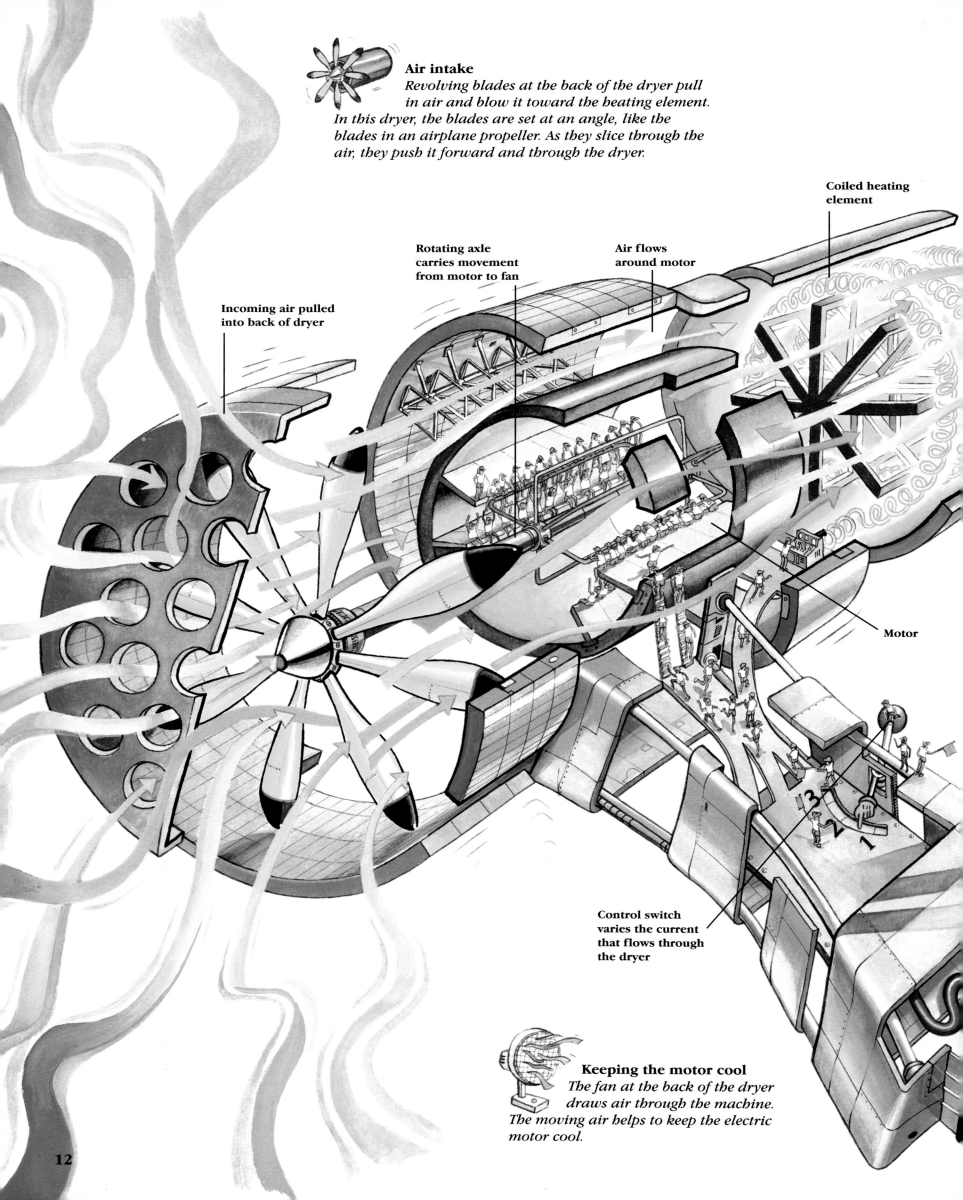

Air intake
Revolving blades at the back of the dryer pull in air and blow it toward the heating element. In this dryer, the blades are set at an angle, like the blades in an airplane propeller. As they slice through the air, they push it forward and through the dryer.

Coiled heating element

Rotating axle carries movement from motor to fan

Air flows around motor

Incoming air pulled into back of dryer

Motor

Control switch varies the current that flows through the dryer

Keeping the motor cool
The fan at the back of the dryer draws air through the machine. The moving air helps to keep the electric motor cool.

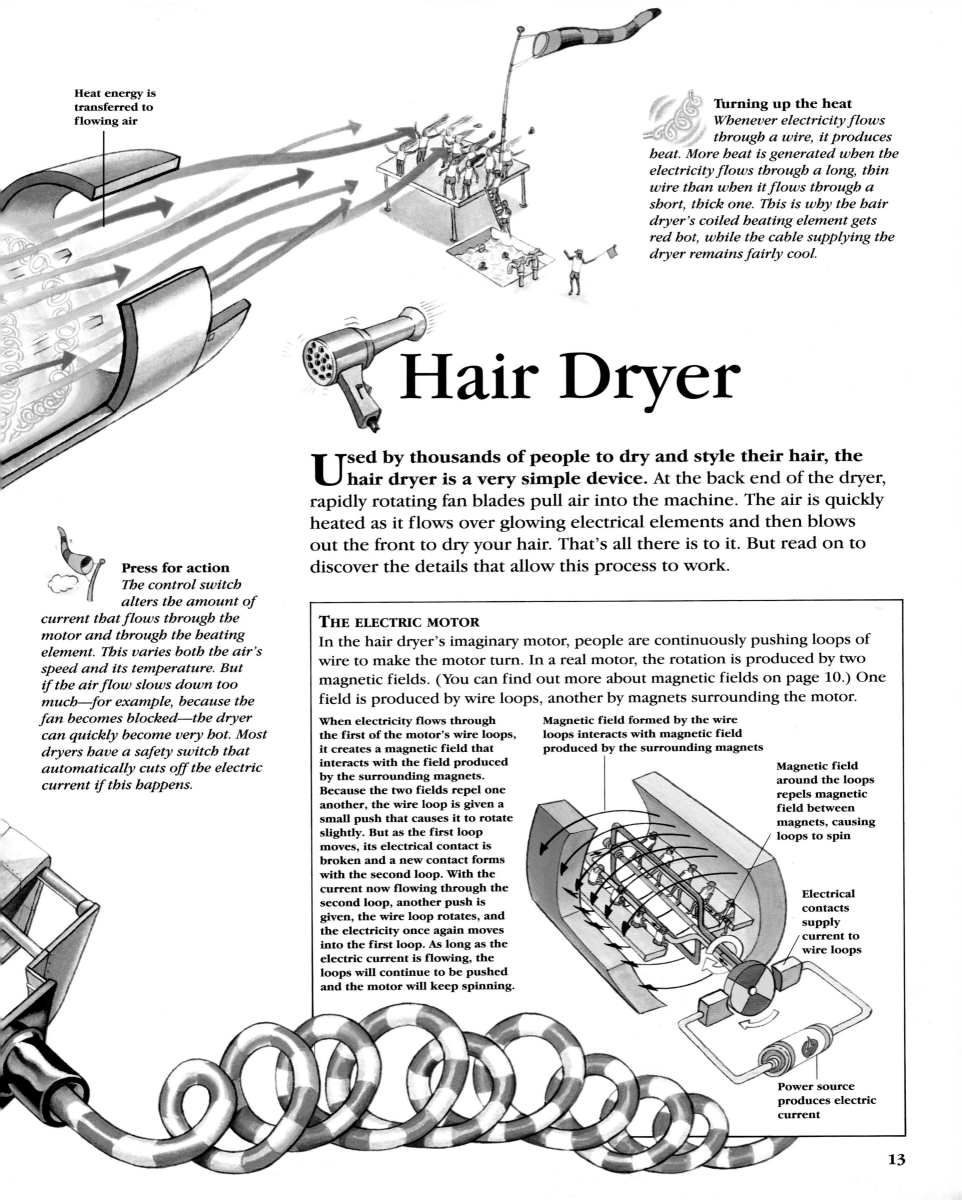

Heat energy is transferred to flowing air

Turning up the heat
Whenever electricity flows through a wire, it produces heat. More heat is generated when the electricity flows through a long, thin wire than when it flows through a short, thick one. This is why the hair dryer's coiled heating element gets red hot, while the cable supplying the dryer remains fairly cool.

Hair Dryer

Used by thousands of people to dry and style their hair, the hair dryer is a very simple device. At the back end of the dryer, rapidly rotating fan blades pull air into the machine. The air is quickly heated as it flows over glowing electrical elements and then blows out the front to dry your hair. That's all there is to it. But read on to discover the details that allow this process to work.

Press for action
The control switch alters the amount of current that flows through the motor and through the heating element. This varies both the air's speed and its temperature. But if the air flow slows down too much—for example, because the fan becomes blocked—the dryer can quickly become very hot. Most dryers have a safety switch that automatically cuts off the electric current if this happens.

THE ELECTRIC MOTOR

In the hair dryer's imaginary motor, people are continuously pushing loops of wire to make the motor turn. In a real motor, the rotation is produced by two magnetic fields. (You can find out more about magnetic fields on page 10.) One field is produced by wire loops, another by magnets surrounding the motor.

When electricity flows through the first of the motor's wire loops, it creates a magnetic field that interacts with the field produced by the surrounding magnets. Because the two fields repel one another, the wire loop is given a small push that causes it to rotate slightly. But as the first loop moves, its electrical contact is broken and a new contact forms with the second loop. With the current now flowing through the second loop, another push is given, the wire loop rotates, and the electricity once again moves into the first loop. As long as the electric current is flowing, the loops will continue to be pushed and the motor will keep spinning.

Magnetic field formed by the wire loops interacts with magnetic field produced by the surrounding magnets

Magnetic field around the loops repels magnetic field between magnets, causing loops to spin

Electrical contacts supply current to wire loops

Power source produces electric current

Vacuum Cleaner

Twenty-four hours a day, an invisible blizzard piles up dust inside our homes. Some of the dust blows in when we open doors or windows, but a lot of it comes from tiny fibers that break away from our clothes and microscopic flakes that wear away from the surface of our skin.

If dust is not cleaned away it quickly builds up on surfaces all over the house. Fortunately, there is an easy way to get rid of it. The vacuum cleaner creates suction that collects these particles of dust, packing them into a bag that can then be thrown away.

Cleaning by suction
The upper part of the vacuum cleaner consists of a compartment that contains a dust bag and filter. The compartment is airtight, but the dust bag contains tiny holes that let air flow through to a fan underneath. When the cleaner is switched on, the fan sucks air out of the compartment, producing a partial vacuum. The resulting suction pulls air and dirt through the dust pipe into the dust bag.

Full of dirt?
Each time the vacuum cleaner is turned on, the dust bag swells up like a balloon. This is because the pressure of the air inside the bag becomes greater than the air pressure around it.

WHAT IS A VACUUM?
A roomful of air contains billions of tiny particles known as atoms. These atoms are constantly on the move, spreading themselves evenly to fill all the space around them. A vacuum contains no atoms at all. It is completely empty space. In the real world, there is no such thing as a true vacuum. This is because everywhere—including outer space—some atoms are present. However, partial vacuums are found in nature, and they are also created by machines such as the vacuum cleaner. A partial vacuum is a space that contains fewer atoms than the one outside it. When a partial vacuum occurs, the surrounding air will immediately rush in to equalize the pressure. In a vacuum cleaner, the air moves through a narrow tube, creating a powerful suction that can be used to pull dust and dirt into the machine.

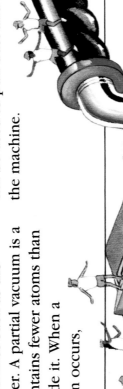

Air outside

Fan

Partial vacuum

Air in dust bag

Dust pipe

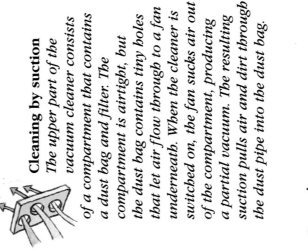

On-off switch

A bagful of dust
The dust bag is made of a special material that allows air to flow through while keeping dust and dirt inside. As the bag fills with dust and dirt, it becomes more difficult for air to flow through. As a result, there is less suction, and the vacuum does not clean as well.

Airtight compartment

Disposable dust bag traps dirt and dust while allowing air to pass through

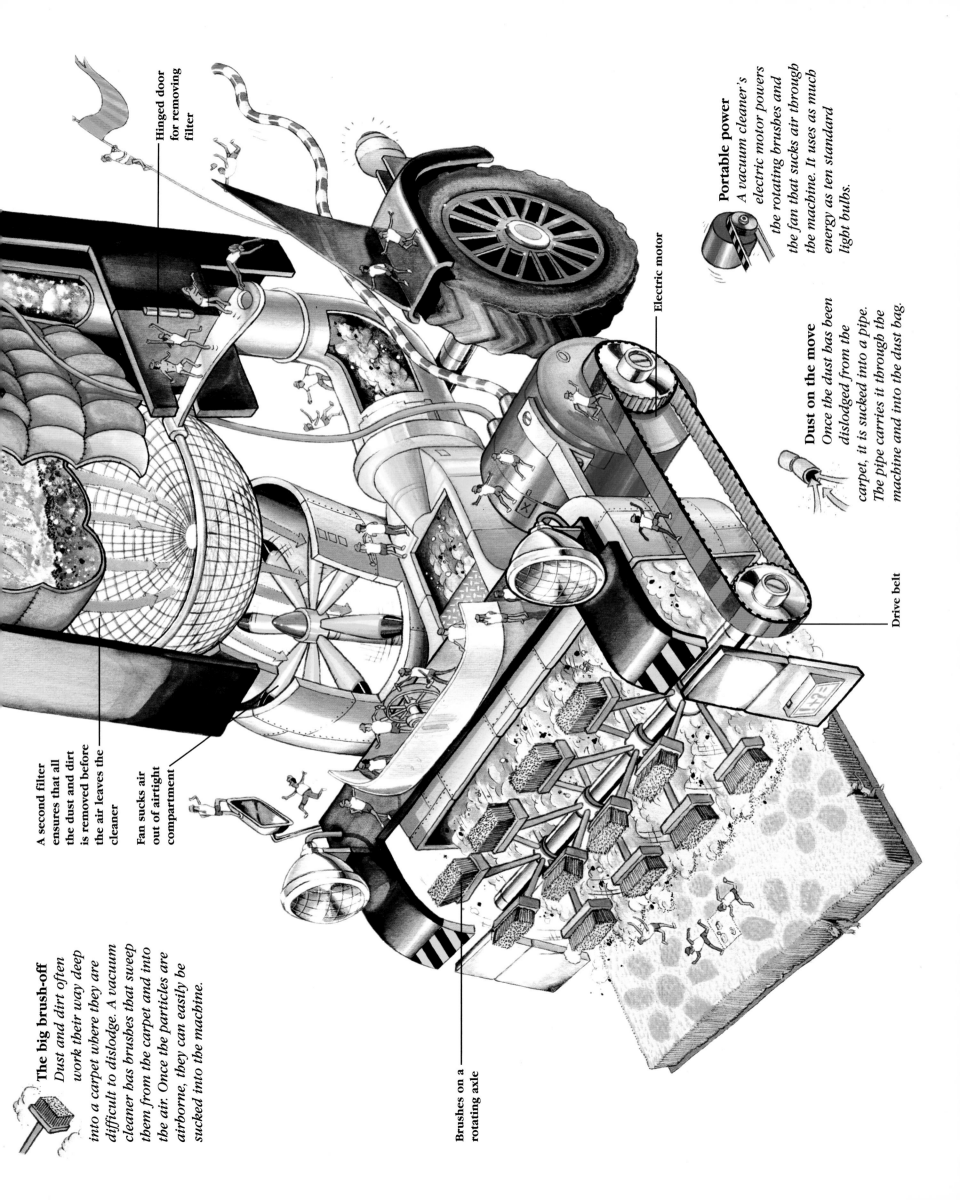

Hinged door for removing filter

Portable power
A vacuum cleaner's electric motor powers the rotating brushes and the fan that sucks air through the machine. It uses as much energy as ten standard light bulbs.

Electric motor

Dust on the move
Once the dust has been dislodged from the carpet, it is sucked into a pipe. The pipe carries it through the machine and into the dust bag.

Drive belt

A second filter ensures that all the dust and dirt is removed before the air leaves the cleaner

Fan sucks air out of airtight compartment

The big brush-off
Dust and dirt often work their way deep into a carpet where they are difficult to dislodge. A vacuum cleaner has brushes that sweep them from the carpet and into the air. Once the particles are airborne, they can easily be sucked into the machine.

Brushes on a rotating axle

Washing Machine

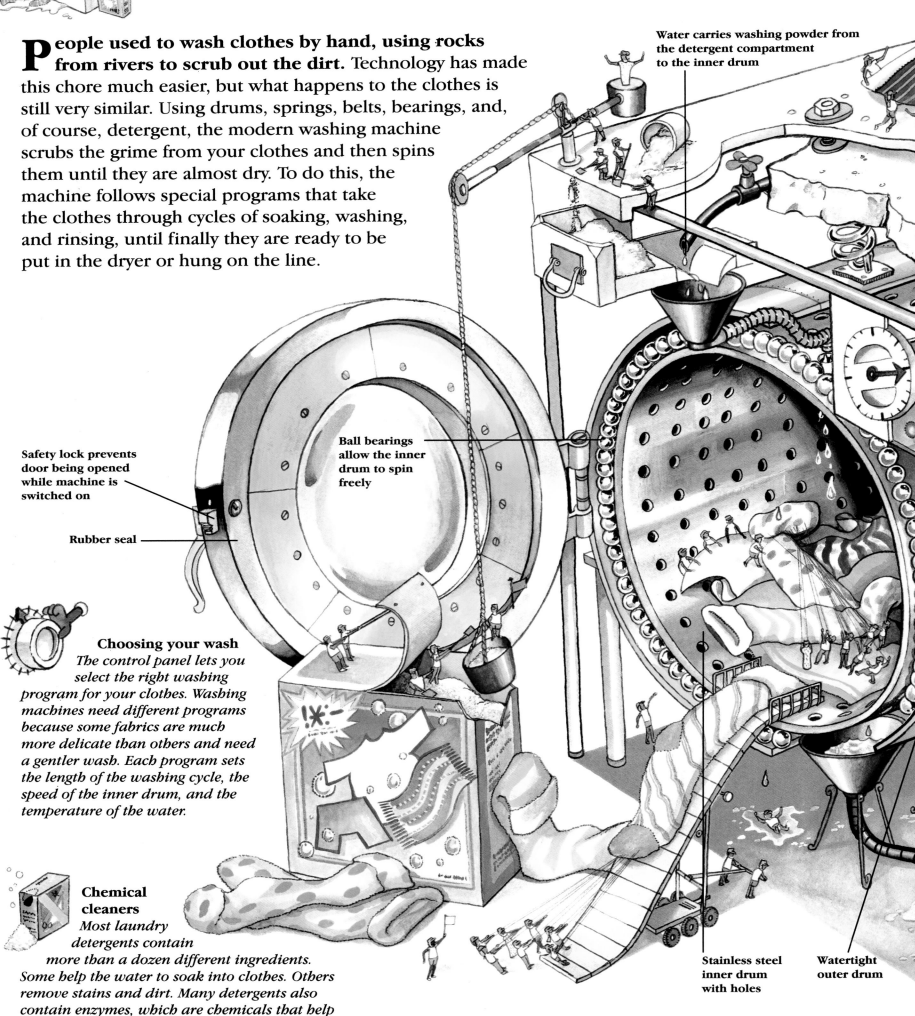

People used to wash clothes by hand, using rocks from rivers to scrub out the dirt. Technology has made this chore much easier, but what happens to the clothes is still very similar. Using drums, springs, belts, bearings, and, of course, detergent, the modern washing machine scrubs the grime from your clothes and then spins them until they are almost dry. To do this, the machine follows special programs that take the clothes through cycles of soaking, washing, and rinsing, until finally they are ready to be put in the dryer or hung on the line.

Water carries washing powder from the detergent compartment to the inner drum

Ball bearings allow the inner drum to spin freely

Safety lock prevents door being opened while machine is switched on

Rubber seal

Choosing your wash
The control panel lets you select the right washing program for your clothes. Washing machines need different programs because some fabrics are much more delicate than others and need a gentler wash. Each program sets the length of the washing cycle, the speed of the inner drum, and the temperature of the water.

Chemical cleaners
Most laundry detergents contain more than a dozen different ingredients. Some help the water to soak into clothes. Others remove stains and dirt. Many detergents also contain enzymes, which are chemicals that help break down substances such as fat or blood.

Stainless steel inner drum with holes

Watertight outer drum

16

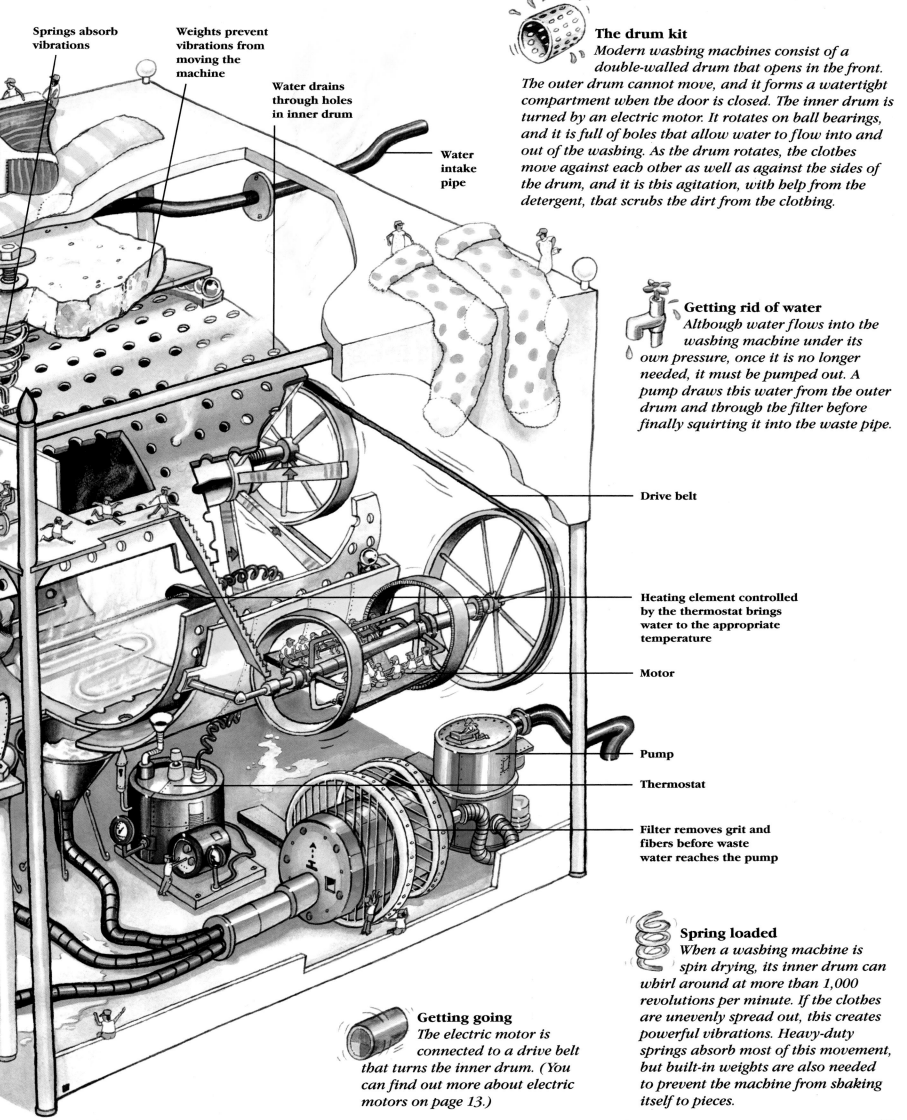

Springs absorb vibrations

Weights prevent vibrations from moving the machine

Water drains through holes in inner drum

Water intake pipe

The drum kit
Modern washing machines consist of a double-walled drum that opens in the front. The outer drum cannot move, and it forms a watertight compartment when the door is closed. The inner drum is turned by an electric motor. It rotates on ball bearings, and it is full of holes that allow water to flow into and out of the washing. As the drum rotates, the clothes move against each other as well as against the sides of the drum, and it is this agitation, with help from the detergent, that scrubs the dirt from the clothing.

Getting rid of water
Although water flows into the washing machine under its own pressure, once it is no longer needed, it must be pumped out. A pump draws this water from the outer drum and through the filter before finally squirting it into the waste pipe.

Drive belt

Heating element controlled by the thermostat brings water to the appropriate temperature

Motor

Pump

Thermostat

Filter removes grit and fibers before waste water reaches the pump

Spring loaded
When a washing machine is spin drying, its inner drum can whirl around at more than 1,000 revolutions per minute. If the clothes are unevenly spread out, this creates powerful vibrations. Heavy-duty springs absorb most of this movement, but built-in weights are also needed to prevent the machine from shaking itself to pieces.

Getting going
The electric motor is connected to a drive belt that turns the inner drum. (You can find out more about electric motors on page 13.)

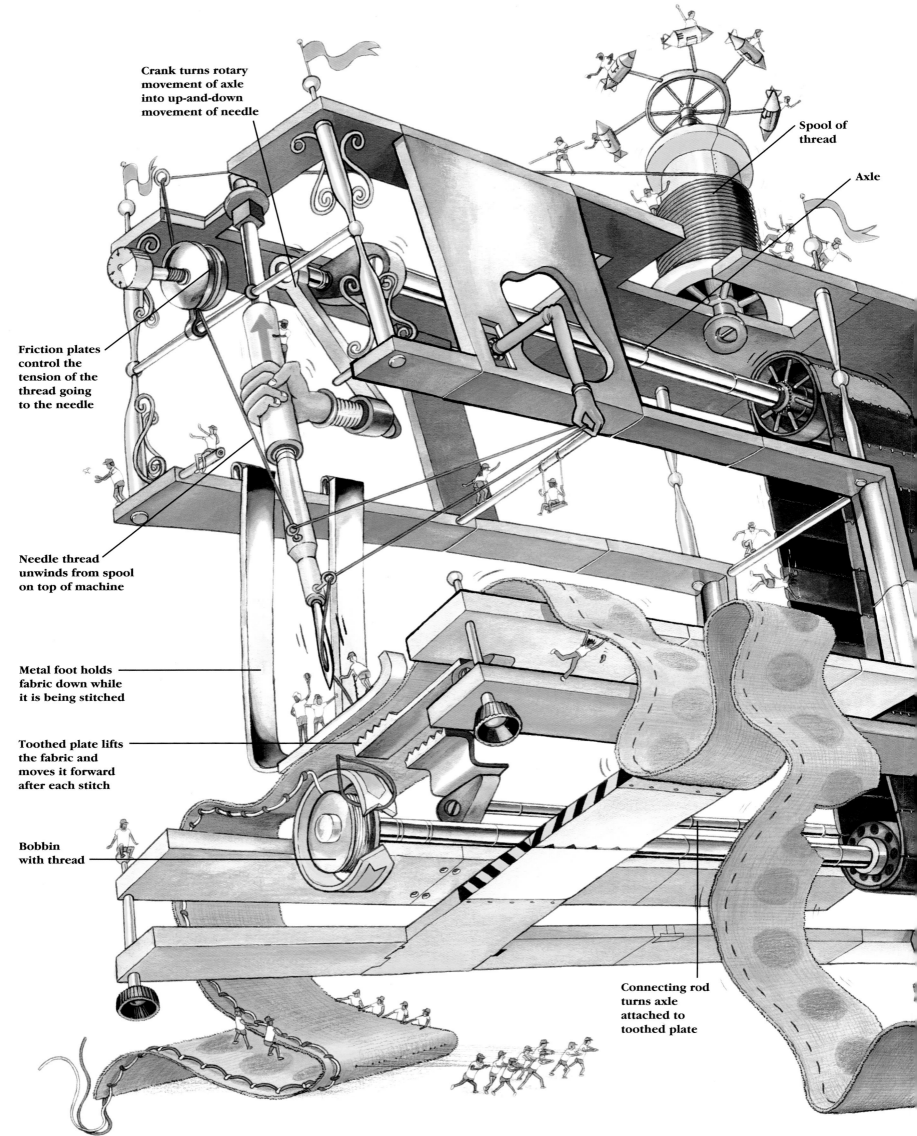

Crank turns rotary movement of axle into up-and-down movement of needle

Friction plates control the tension of the thread going to the needle

Needle thread unwinds from spool on top of machine

Metal foot holds fabric down while it is being stitched

Toothed plate lifts the fabric and moves it forward after each stitch

Bobbin with thread

Spool of thread

Axle

Connecting rod turns axle attached to toothed plate

Sewing Machine

The inside of a sewing machine is like a frantic factory, where many things are happening at once. Axles spin, belts hum, rods clatter, and the needle moves up and down with blinding speed. But behind this seeming chaos is a series of carefully designed movements, all powered by a single electric motor. In less time than it takes you to blink, a sewing machine makes a stitch, tightens it, and moves the fabric forward in preparation for the next stitch.

Making things move
Sewing machines today are powered by small electric motors. (To find out more about electric motors, see page 13.) The motor turns an axle that is linked to the rest of the moving parts within the sewing machine. Devices called cranks and cams are used to convert the rotational movement of the axle into the up-and-down movement of the needle.

Tightening up
Before the thread reaches the needle it travels between two coin-shaped friction plates. These adjustable plates are held together by a screw and a spring, and they control the tension of the thread. By increasing the pressure between the plates, the stitches become tighter.

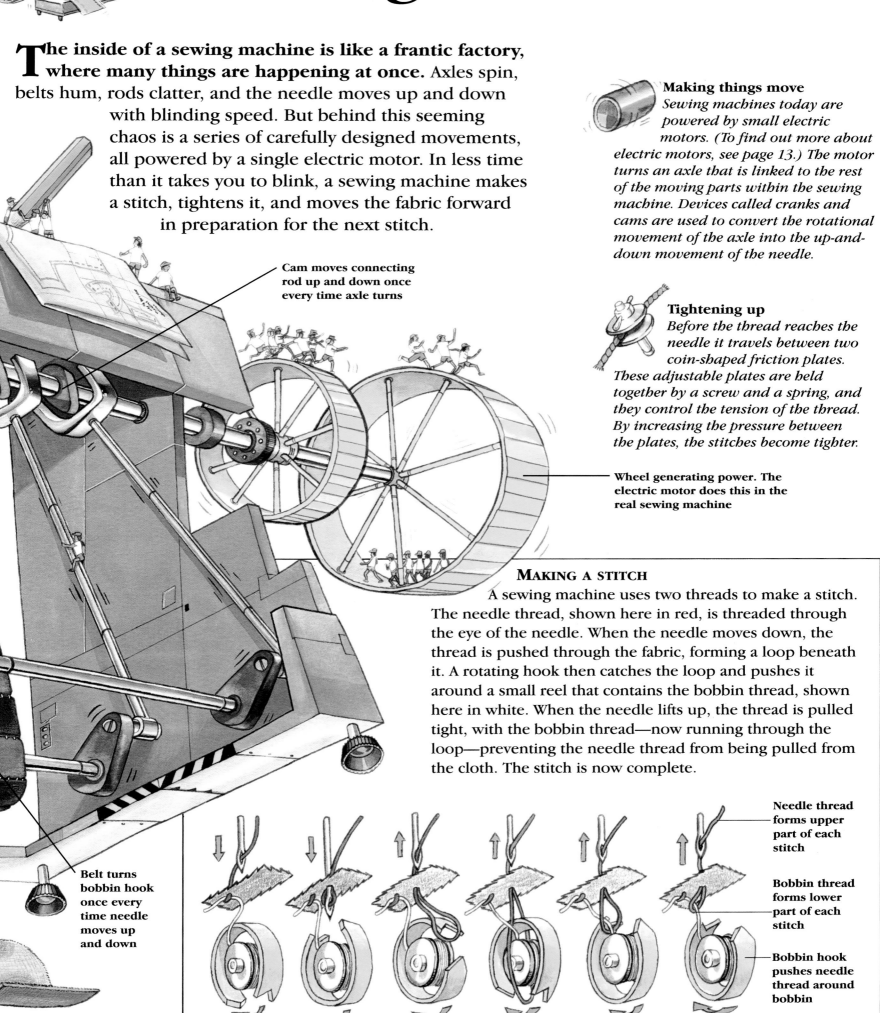

Cam moves connecting rod up and down once every time axle turns

Wheel generating power. The electric motor does this in the real sewing machine

Belt turns bobbin hook once every time needle moves up and down

MAKING A STITCH
A sewing machine uses two threads to make a stitch. The needle thread, shown here in red, is threaded through the eye of the needle. When the needle moves down, the thread is pushed through the fabric, forming a loop beneath it. A rotating hook then catches the loop and pushes it around a small reel that contains the bobbin thread, shown here in white. When the needle lifts up, the thread is pulled tight, with the bobbin thread—now running through the loop—preventing the needle thread from being pulled from the cloth. The stitch is now complete.

Needle thread forms upper part of each stitch

Bobbin thread forms lower part of each stitch

Bobbin hook pushes needle thread around bobbin

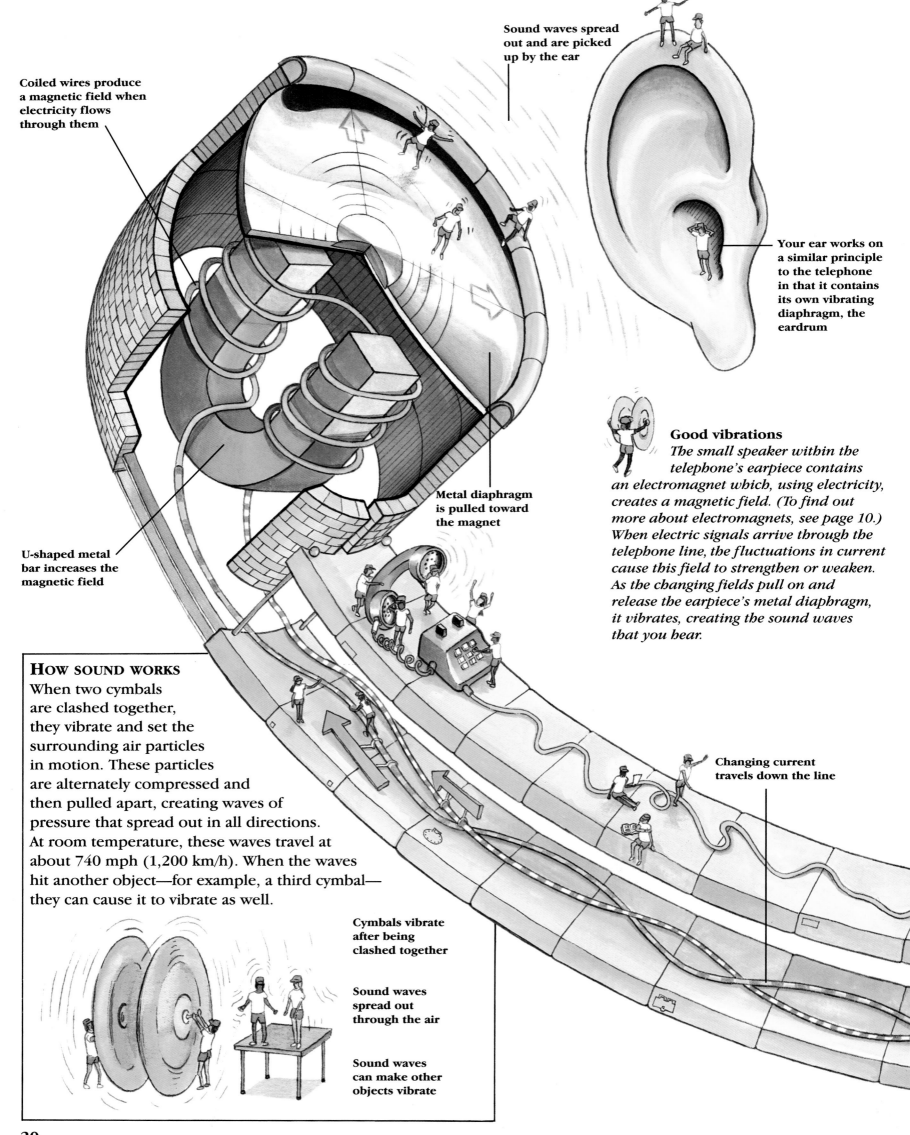

Coiled wires produce a magnetic field when electricity flows through them

Sound waves spread out and are picked up by the ear

Your ear works on a similar principle to the telephone in that it contains its own vibrating diaphragm, the eardrum

Metal diaphragm is pulled toward the magnet

U-shaped metal bar increases the magnetic field

Good vibrations
The small speaker within the telephone's earpiece contains an electromagnet which, using electricity, creates a magnetic field. (To find out more about electromagnets, see page 10.) When electric signals arrive through the telephone line, the fluctuations in current cause this field to strengthen or weaken. As the changing fields pull on and release the earpiece's metal diaphragm, it vibrates, creating the sound waves that you hear.

HOW SOUND WORKS
When two cymbals are clashed together, they vibrate and set the surrounding air particles in motion. These particles are alternately compressed and then pulled apart, creating waves of pressure that spread out in all directions. At room temperature, these waves travel at about 740 mph (1,200 km/h). When the waves hit another object—for example, a third cymbal—they can cause it to vibrate as well.

Changing current travels down the line

Cymbals vibrate after being clashed together

Sound waves spread out through the air

Sound waves can make other objects vibrate

Telephone

Although telephones come in different shapes and sizes, they all use similar principles to function. Whenever you talk, you send waves of pressure through the air. If you whisper, the air does not move much, but if you shout, it really gets going. A telephone's mouthpiece picks up these waves and converts them into a fluctuating electrical current. The current is sent down the telephone line, ending up at the number you have dialed. Here, the electrical energy is converted back into movement, or sound waves, and the person on the other end hears you talking. With the reply, the whole process repeats itself, only in the opposite direction.

Talking
By forcing wind through your voice box (larynx), you can make sound waves in the air. These waves are then picked up by your ear and interpreted by your brain as words.

Carbon microphone
The microphone in many telephones contains particles of carbon. These particles conduct electricity, and they do this best if they are given a good squeeze. Loud sounds squeeze the particles more than soft ones, thus producing larger changes in the current that is transmitted down the telephone line.

Sensing sound
A telephone's mouthpiece contains a small disk, or diaphragm, which vibrates when you talk. The diaphragm is connected to a microphone. The microphone converts the diaphragm's movement into a fluctuating electrical current that travels down the telephone line.

Diaphragm is vibrated by sound waves

Loud sounds cause more carbon particles to be squeezed

Cable connecting handset to telephone and outside line

The strength of current that flows depends on the number of carbon particles that are squeezed

Toilet Tank

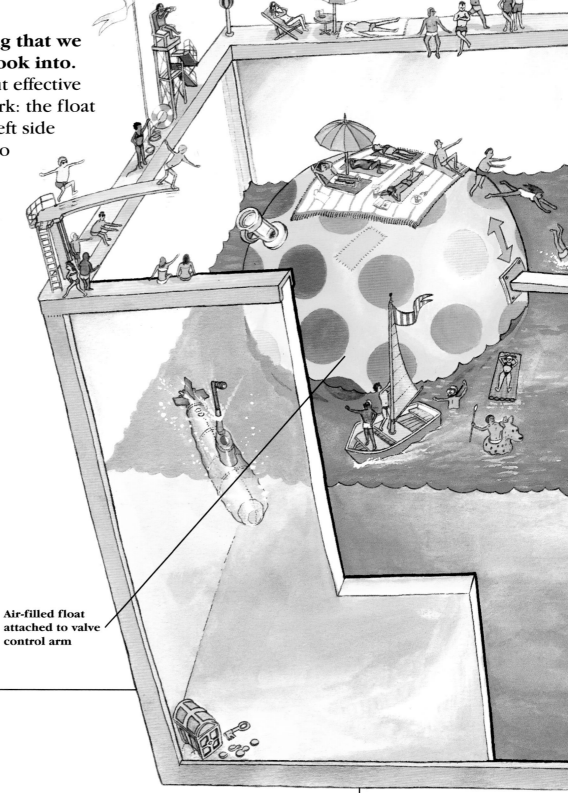

The toilet tank is something that we see every day but rarely look into. Inside the tank are two simple but effective devices that allow the toilet to work: the float and the siphon. The float, seen on the left side of the tank, ensures that the water fills to the proper level, and no higher. In the center of the tank is a device that draws the water into the toilet in a continuous flow. This is the siphon. Now take the plunge and find out more about what happens when you flush the toilet.

Making water move

The toilet handle is connected to a metal disk, with holes in it, at the base of the siphon. Above this is a smaller sliding disk with no holes in it. When you push on the handle the disks are forced up together, so the holes in the lower disk are closed. As the disks slide upward, they force water through the siphon. Once the water is flowing around the bend, the rest of the water in the tank follows. It is sucked through the holes in the lower disk, which by now has settled back to the bottom of the siphon bell, and around the edges of the upper one. If the toilet siphon had only one disk—the one with the holes—it would be hard to start the siphon working. When the handle is pushed, most of the water would escape through the holes, instead of being forced upward.

Air-filled float attached to valve control arm

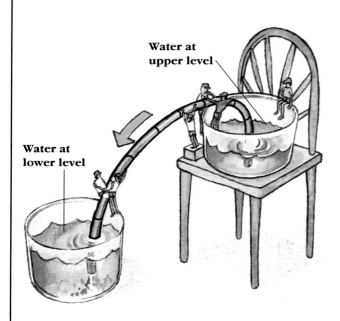

Water at upper level

Water at lower level

WHY SIPHONS WORK

When liquid is forced up a short length of tubing and then down a longer length, the resulting suction causes a continuous flow of water to follow. For this to occur, however, not only must the siphon tube remain full of water, but the water must move from a higher to a lower level. This is what allows the unbroken flow of water into the toilet bowl. Were air to enter the siphon tube, the suction would be broken and the water would come to a halt.

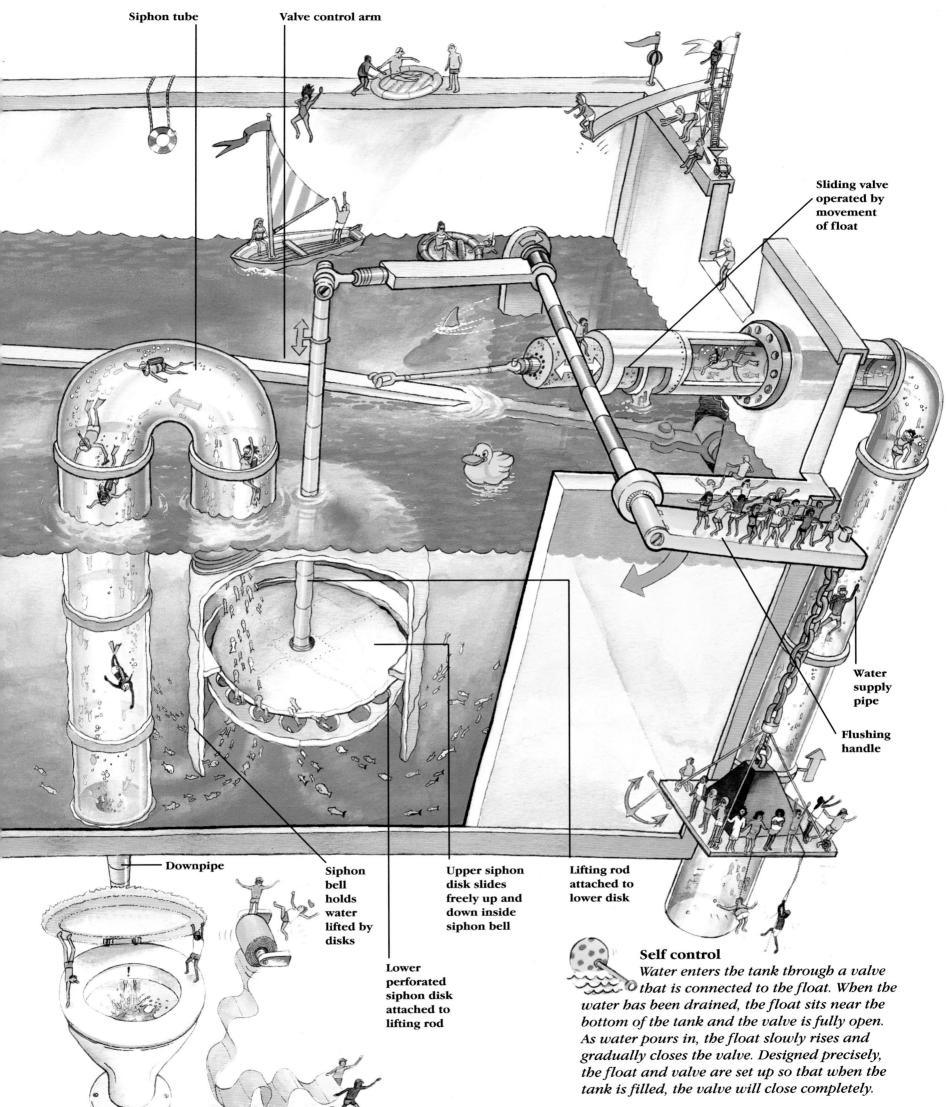

Siphon tube

Valve control arm

Sliding valve operated by movement of float

Water supply pipe

Flushing handle

Downpipe

Siphon bell holds water lifted by disks

Upper siphon disk slides freely up and down inside siphon bell

Lifting rod attached to lower disk

Lower perforated siphon disk attached to lifting rod

Self control

Water enters the tank through a valve that is connected to the float. When the water has been drained, the float sits near the bottom of the tank and the valve is fully open. As water pours in, the float slowly rises and gradually closes the valve. Designed precisely, the float and valve are set up so that when the tank is filled, the valve will close completely.

23

Toaster

For breakfast lovers, this could be one of the most important machines ever invented. It toasts bread to perfection and automatically turns off when the slices are ready to eat.

This cut-away toaster will help answer one of the most pressing questions facing any toast enthusiast: how does the toaster know when the toast is done? The answer lies in a tiny device called a bimetallic strip, which responds to heat by changing shape. The strip is set to release a catch at just the right moment, popping up the toast and preventing it from burning.

Timed to perfection
Some toasters are controlled by a timer instead of a bimetallic strip. When the timer reaches zero, it activates a switch that turns on the electromagnet. (To find out more about electromagnets, see page 10.)

Ready for lift off
When you put bread in the toaster and push down the handle, you stretch a pair of metal springs. This causes a catch near the handle to engage with a hinged metal bar, and the bread is held in position. When the toast is ready, the metal bar is released, the springs contract, and the toast shoots skyward.

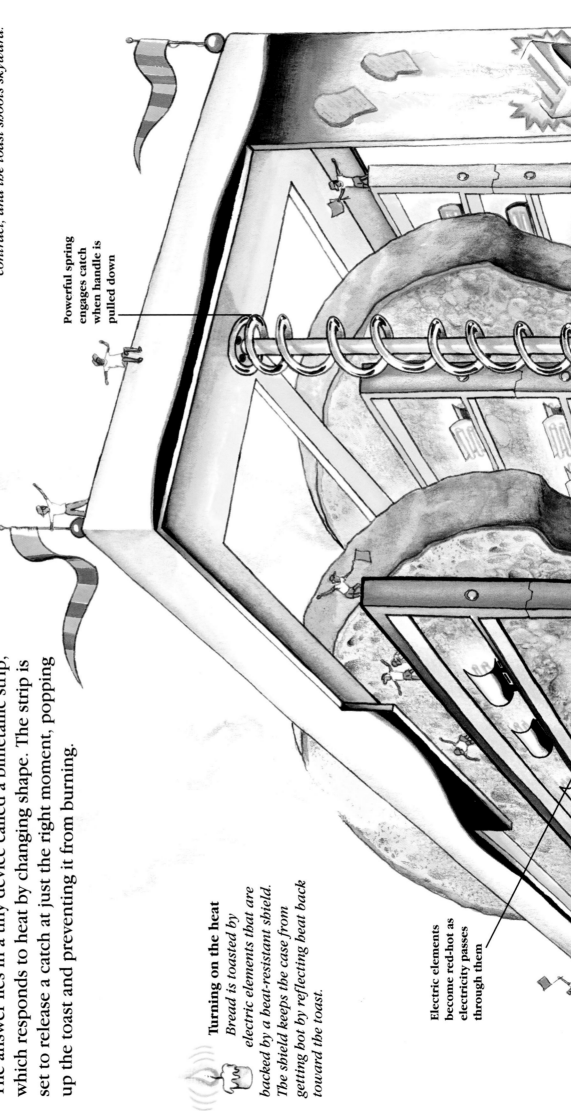

Powerful spring engages catch when handle is pulled down

Electric elements become red-hot as electricity passes through them

Turning on the heat
Bread is toasted by electric elements that are backed by a heat-resistant shield. The shield keeps the case from getting hot by reflecting heat back toward the toast.

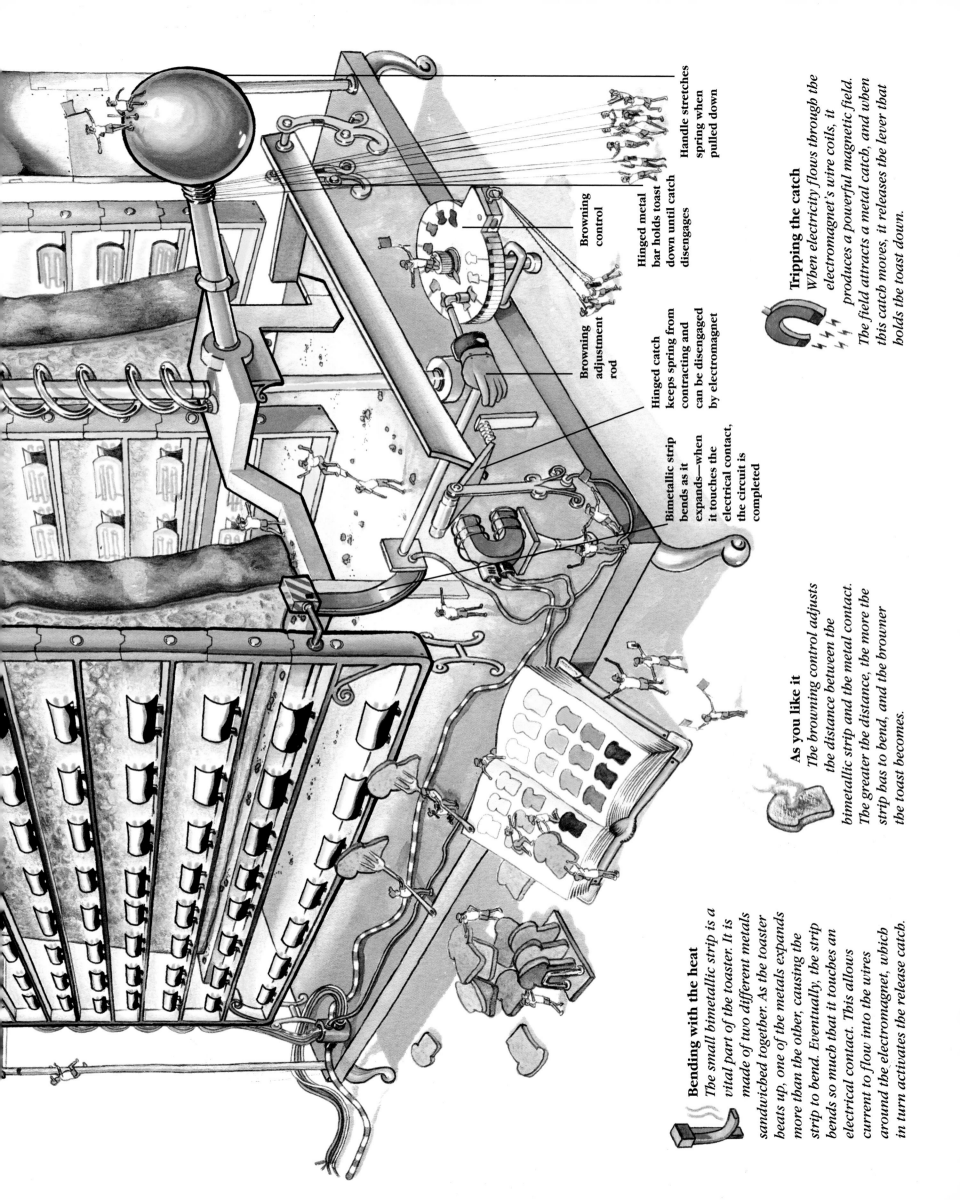

Handle stretches spring when pulled down

Hinged metal bar holds toast down until catch disengages

Browning control

Browning adjustment rod

Hinged catch keeps spring from contracting and can be disengaged by electromagnet

Bimetallic strip bends as it expands—when it touches the electrical contact, the circuit is completed

Tripping the catch
When electricity flows through the electromagnet's wire coils, it produces a powerful magnetic field. The field attracts a metal catch, and when this catch moves, it releases the lever that holds the toast down.

As you like it
The browning control adjusts the distance between the bimetallic strip and the metal contact. The greater the distance, the more the strip has to bend, and the browner the toast becomes.

Bending with the heat
The small bimetallic strip is a vital part of the toaster. It is made of two different metals sandwiched together. As the toaster heats up, one of the metals expands more than the other, causing the strip to bend. Eventually, the strip bends so much that it touches an electrical contact. This allows current to flow into the wires around the electromagnet, which in turn activates the release catch.

Food Processor

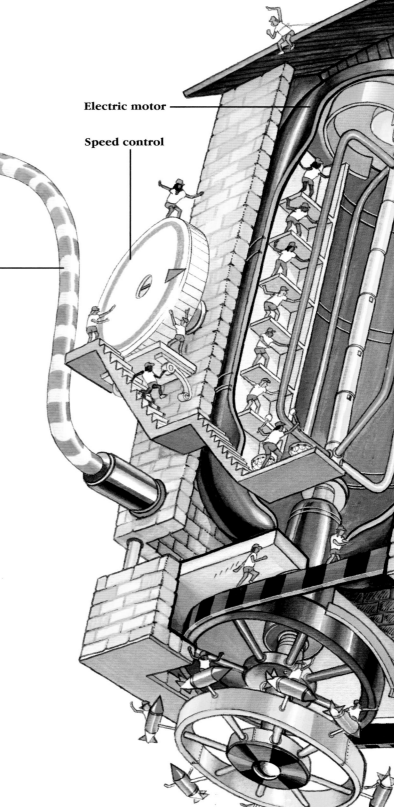

When preparing food, many jobs can take a very long time if done by hand: for example, grating cheese, mixing batter, or slicing carrots. With the invention of the food processor, work in the kitchen can now be done much quicker and with far more efficiency. Food can be chopped, liquified, kneaded, mixed, or sliced in only seconds.

Because of its sharp attachments and rapidly moving parts, a food processor also has the potential to be dangerous. Fortunately, most food processors include a simple device that prevents accidents from occurring. The lid of each processor contains a catch that connects to a safety switch. If the lid is on and fastened tightly, the switch allows electricity to flow through the motor. But if the lid has been removed, or if it is not positioned correctly, the motor will not turn on.

Turning on the power
The food processor uses an electric motor to make things move. Although its motor produces only about one-hundredth of the power of a car's engine, it has plenty of power to chop up almost any food.

Controlling the speed
The motor's speed is determined by the strength of the electric current that flows through it. When the control knob is set at the slowest speed, only a weak current flows through the motor. When the knob is set at the highest speed, the current is much stronger and the motor moves more rapidly.

Electric motor

Speed control

Power supply

DIFFERENT TOOLS FOR DIFFERENT TASKS
A food processor is supplied with a range of attachments that can be used to chop, slice, or blend different kinds of food.

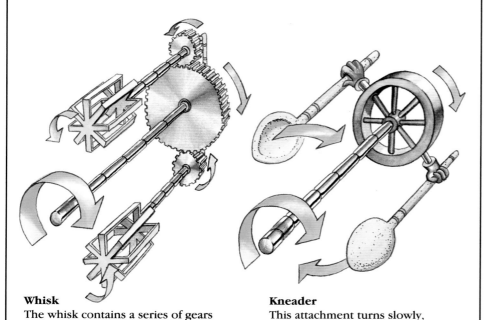

Whisk
The whisk contains a series of gears that make it turn very quickly. As it spins, it folds a lot of air into the food. The whisk is used to whip cream or egg whites.

Kneader
This attachment turns slowly, beating a flour and liquid mixture to make dough. The kneader is also used for folding ingredients into one another.

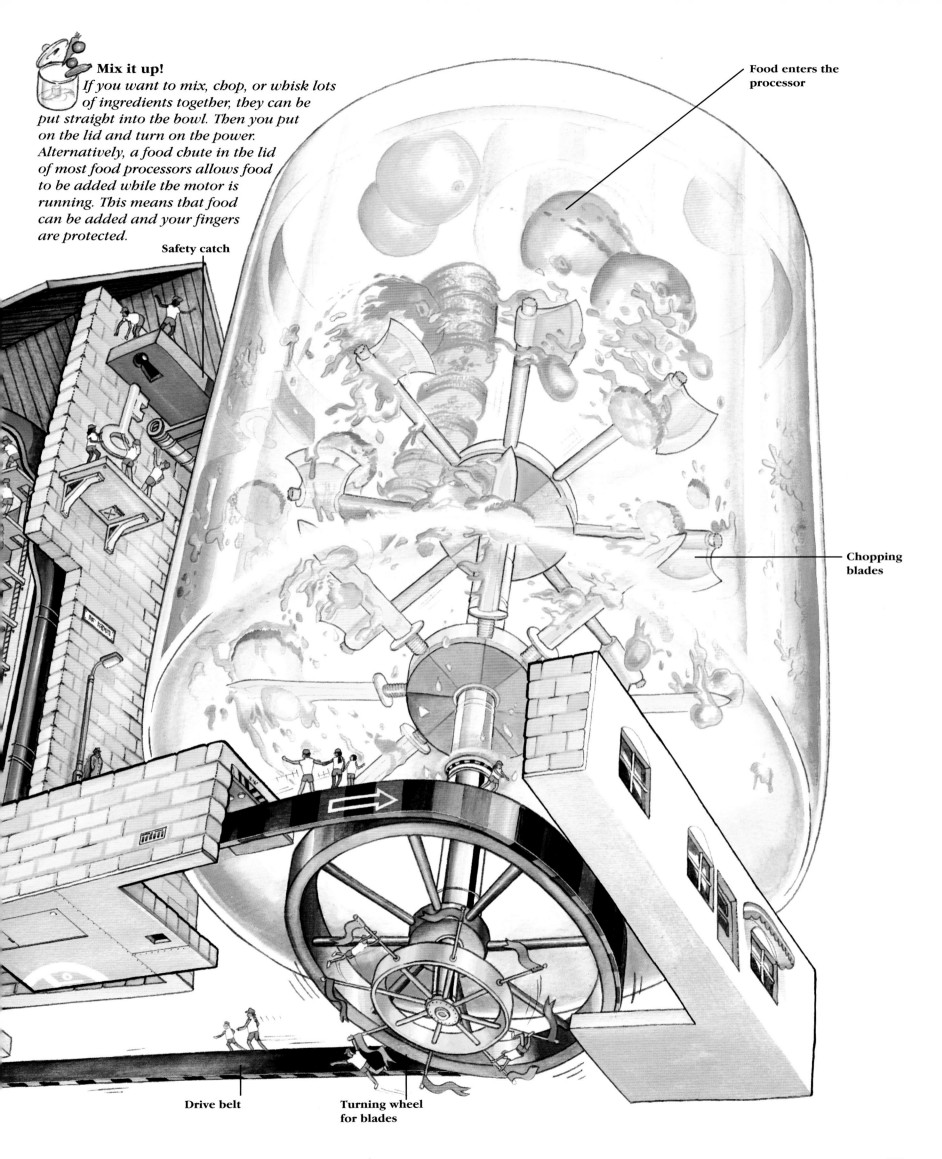

Mix it up!

If you want to mix, chop, or whisk lots of ingredients together, they can be put straight into the bowl. Then you put on the lid and turn on the power. Alternatively, a food chute in the lid of most food processors allows food to be added while the motor is running. This means that food can be added and your fingers are protected.

Food enters the processor

Safety catch

Chopping blades

Drive belt

Turning wheel for blades

Microwave Oven

To many people, microwave ovens are a mystery. Unlike conventional ovens, they heat food without getting hot themselves, and they complete the cooking in a fraction of the time that is normally required.

The secret of this rapid cooking lies in a gun-like device called a magnetron. When the oven is turned on, microwaves are fired from the magnetron at a moving fan that scatters them in all directions. Although the microwaves bounce off the walls of the oven, they pass straight through food. When these waves interact with moisture inside the food, water molecules begin to move rapidly. This motion generates heat, cooking the food.

What are microwaves?
Microwaves are a form of energy similar to light. They travel at 186,000 mph (300,000 km/h), and can pass through air, food, or empty space. Microwaves reach us all the time from space, but they are so weak that they have no effect on us. The microwaves used in ovens are much more powerful.

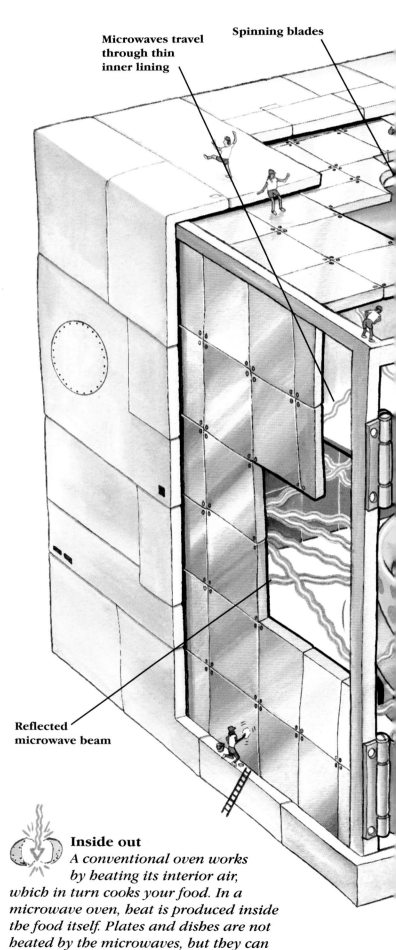

Microwaves travel through thin inner lining

Spinning blades

Reflected microwave beam

1. Cold

1. In cold food, water molecules are spread out randomly. They move about, but only slowly.

COOKING WITH WAVES
The water molecules in food are situated randomly. But when microwave energy passes through the food, the molecules instantly begin moving at the same time. First they point one way and then they flip around to face the opposite direction. The action is then repeated. This rapid movement back and forth produces heat.

2. Warm

2. When microwaves start to travel through the food, the water molecules begin to jostle very rapidly as the waves make them flip first in one direction and then the other.

3. Hot

3. This rapid jostling produces heat. The heat quickly spreads through the food, cooking it in an extremely short amount of time.

Inside out
A conventional oven works by heating its interior air, which in turn cooks your food. In a microwave oven, heat is produced inside the food itself. Plates and dishes are not heated by the microwaves, but they can warm up through contact with the food.

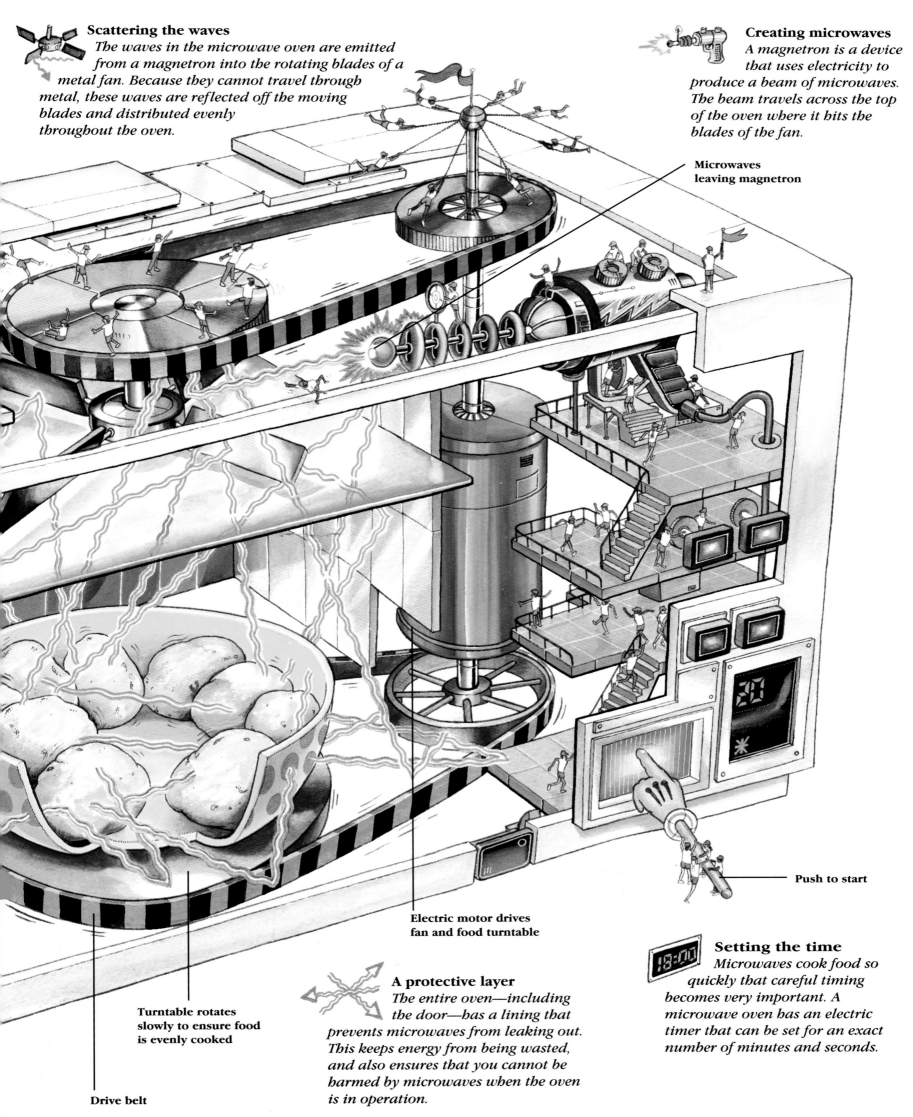

Scattering the waves
The waves in the microwave oven are emitted from a magnetron into the rotating blades of a metal fan. Because they cannot travel through metal, these waves are reflected off the moving blades and distributed evenly throughout the oven.

Creating microwaves
A magnetron is a device that uses electricity to produce a beam of microwaves. The beam travels across the top of the oven where it hits the blades of the fan.

Microwaves leaving magnetron

Push to start

Electric motor drives fan and food turntable

Turntable rotates slowly to ensure food is evenly cooked

Drive belt

A protective layer
The entire oven—including the door—has a lining that prevents microwaves from leaking out. This keeps energy from being wasted, and also ensures that you cannot be harmed by microwaves when the oven is in operation.

Setting the time
Microwaves cook food so quickly that careful timing becomes very important. A microwave oven has an electric timer that can be set for an exact number of minutes and seconds.

Refrigerator

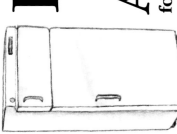

An important machine in any home, the **refrigerator is essential in keeping many foods from spoiling.** Normally, the back of it is against the wall, hiding the working parts. But this refrigerator has been turned around—so you can see exactly how your food is kept cold.

A refrigerator works by taking heat from its interior and carrying it outside. It does this by pumping a special fluid, called a refrigerant, through a long loop of piping. During each journey through the loop, the refrigerant changes from a liquid into a vapor, and then back to a liquid. As it becomes a vapor, the refrigerant absorbs heat from the food inside the refrigerator. Then it is turned back into a liquid and releases heat into the kitchen.

Into the interior

When the refrigerant enters the freezer, it moves through a narrow nozzle, called an expansion valve, into a series of pipes. These allow the liquid to expand into a vapor as heat is absorbed from inside the freezer compartment and the refrigerator. When this occurs, the refrigerator's interior cools and its contents become cold.

Bad news for germs

No matter how clean your kitchen is, there will always be some germs on your food. In warm conditions, germs grow rapidly, and they can cause food to go bad quickly. In a refrigerator, where the temperature is much lower, germs grow more slowly, so food stays fresh longer.

Keeping cool

If you go for a swim and then come out without drying off, you will soon start to cool down. This happens as the water on your skin begins to evaporate (turn to vapor). For this to happen, heat is required. The water gets this heat from your body, and you begin to feel cold because heat is being taken away from you. In the same way, the interior of a refrigerator becomes cold as it gives up heat. This heat is used to turn liquid refrigerant into vapor.

Staying at the right temperature

The compressor is controlled by a thermostat—a device that regulates temperature. The compressor starts pumping when the refrigerator's temperature starts to rise, and it stops when the refrigerator cools to the desired degree.

Narrow nozzle, or expansion valve

Freezer

Refrigerant expands into these pipes, becoming a vapor and taking heat out of the refrigerator

Refrigerant flowing out to the piping

Pipes around freezer

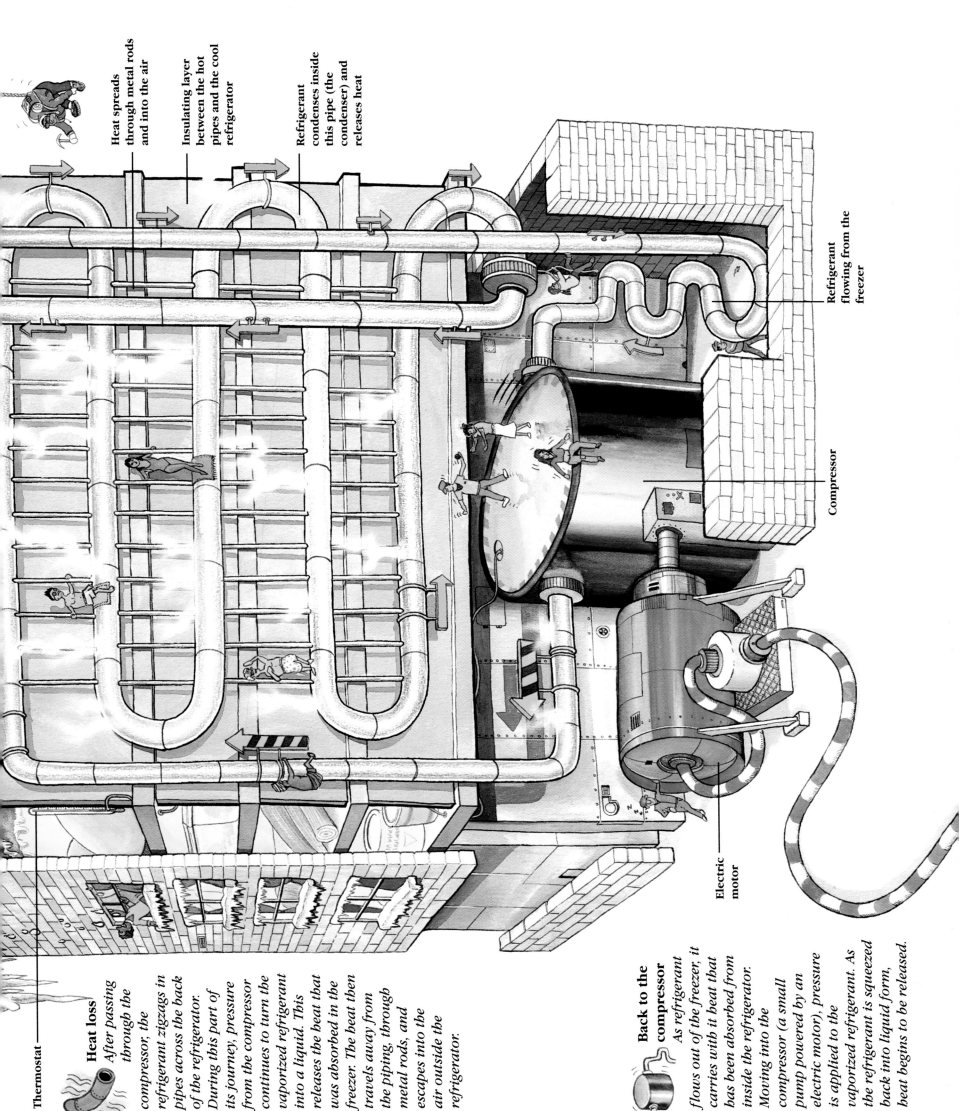

Heat spreads through metal rods and into the air

Insulating layer between the hot pipes and the cool refrigerator

Refrigerant condenses inside this pipe (the condenser) and releases heat

Refrigerant flowing from the freezer

Compressor

Electric motor

Thermostat

Heat loss
After passing through the compressor, the refrigerant zigzags in pipes across the back of the refrigerator. During this part of its journey, pressure from the compressor continues to turn the vaporized refrigerant into a liquid. This releases the heat that was absorbed in the freezer. The heat then travels away from the piping, through metal rods, and escapes into the air outside the refrigerator.

Back to the compressor
As refrigerant flows out of the freezer, it carries with it heat that has been absorbed from inside the refrigerator. Moving into the compressor (a small pump powered by an electric motor), pressure is applied to the vaporized refrigerant. As the refrigerant is squeezed back into liquid form, heat begins to be released.

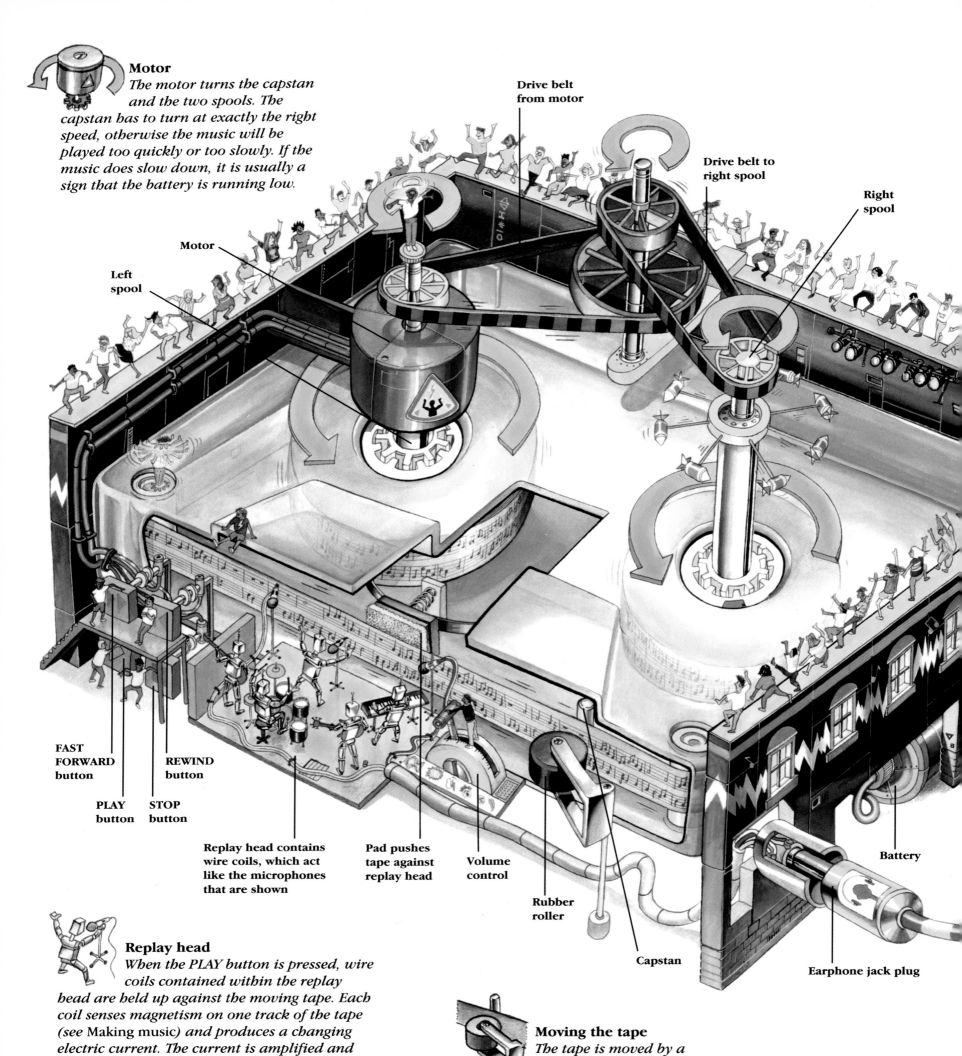

Motor
The motor turns the capstan and the two spools. The capstan has to turn at exactly the right speed, otherwise the music will be played too quickly or too slowly. If the music does slow down, it is usually a sign that the battery is running low.

Drive belt from motor

Drive belt to right spool

Right spool

Motor

Left spool

FAST FORWARD button

PLAY button

STOP button

REWIND button

Replay head contains wire coils, which act like the microphones that are shown

Pad pushes tape against replay head

Volume control

Rubber roller

Capstan

Battery

Earphone jack plug

Replay head
When the PLAY button is pressed, wire coils contained within the replay head are held up against the moving tape. Each coil senses magnetism on one track of the tape (see *Making music*) and produces a changing electric current. The current is amplified and then sent to one of the earphones.

Moving the tape
The tape is moved by a revolving capstan, which is a metal pin powered by the motor. When you push the PLAY button, a rubber roller presses the tape against the pin, and the tape begins to move.

32

Music on tape
A tape is made of a thin ribbon of plastic, covered with particles that can be magnetized. If the tape is blank, the particles are randomly scattered, so all you hear is a hiss. If the tape has been recorded, the particles are magnetized in a pattern that the replay head can translate into the music that you hear.

Left earphone

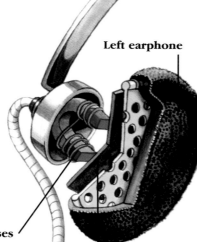

Making music
When you listen to live music, you hear a slightly different mixture of sounds in each ear. A stereo tape recording reproduces this effect by having two different tracks, or recordings, running at the same time. Each track is played through a different earphone.

Electromagnet uses the electrical current to make the diaphragm vibrate

Electrical cable leading to earphones

Diaphragm produces sound waves (see page 20 for a more detailed explanation)

Right earphone

Personal Stereo

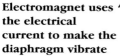

How many sides?
You may be surprised to discover that a tape has just one working side, and this always faces outward. The replay head reads only half the width of the tape, so two recordings can be fitted on side by side. The two recordings run in opposite directions.

Collecting the tape
Once the tape has moved past the capstan, it is wound onto a spool. Unlike the capstan, the spool changes speed as the tape plays. It turns very quickly when it is empty, but it slows down as it fills up. This ensures that the tape always travels at the same speed. If you press the FAST FORWARD button, the capstan disengages, the motor speeds up, and the tape winds rapidly onto the spool.

How can you get a complete musical band, with all its instruments, into a box that is small enough to clip onto your belt? The answer, of course, is you can't. But with the help of modern electronics, you can have the next best thing—a personal stereo that plays any kind of music you wish.

Like other tape recorders, a personal stereo works by sensing magnetized particles on a tape. When there is no music on a tape the metal particles on it are unmagnetized and lie in a random pattern. On a recorded tape, however, the particles have been magnetized in an order that can be translated into electrical impulses. The magnetized particles are detected by tiny wire coils in the replay head, and (using power from a battery) these produce a changing electric current. The earphones then convert the current into sound waves by way of a mechanical diaphragm, and you are able to hear your favorite band—any time you want!

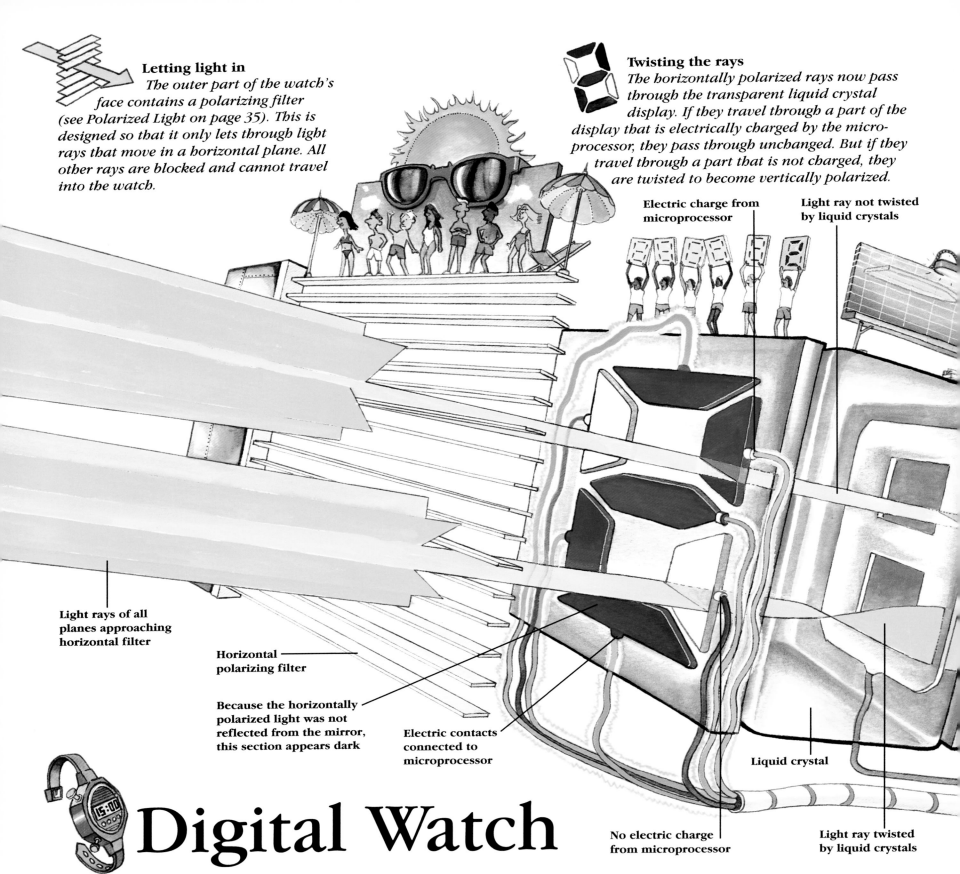

Letting light in
The outer part of the watch's face contains a polarizing filter (see Polarized Light on page 35). This is designed so that it only lets through light rays that move in a horizontal plane. All other rays are blocked and cannot travel into the watch.

Twisting the rays
The horizontally polarized rays now pass through the transparent liquid crystal display. If they travel through a part of the display that is electrically charged by the microprocessor, they pass through unchanged. But if they travel through a part that is not charged, they are twisted to become vertically polarized.

Electric charge from microprocessor

Light ray not twisted by liquid crystals

Light rays of all planes approaching horizontal filter

Horizontal polarizing filter

Because the horizontally polarized light was not reflected from the mirror, this section appears dark

Electric contacts connected to microprocessor

Liquid crystal

No electric charge from microprocessor

Light ray twisted by liquid crystals

Digital Watch

A digital watch is like an electronic sandwich. Although it is just a fraction of an inch thick, it contains many different layers pressed closely together. Here, the layers have been separated so you can see the role that each plays in making the watch function.

Unlike a mechanical watch, a digital watch is extremely accurate. At its heart is a microscopic crystal. When connected to an electric circuit, the crystal produces pulses of electricity at a very precise rate. A microprocessor uses these pulses to calculate the correct time. To find out how the time is displayed, follow the rays of light into the watch and then back out again.

Liquid crystal display
Liquid crystals have an unusual effect on light. Normally, these special crystals "twist" polarized light, so its plane of polarization changes by 90 degrees. In this manner, a horizontal ray of light turns to become vertical, and is able to pass through a vertical filter. However, if an electric charge is passed across the crystals, they alter and no longer twist light. In a watch, the crystals are sandwiched between electric contacts, and the microprocessor uses tiny electric charges to control them so that numbers appear on the display.

Blocking the way

The vertical filter only lets through light rays that move in a vertical plane. The rays that have been twisted by the liquid crystal display are now vertically polarized and can get through. But the rays that have not been twisted cannot pass through.

Bouncing back

If a ray of light passes through the vertical polarizing filter, it reaches a mirror. It is then reflected back through the display and out of the watch, making the display look silvery or white. But if an incoming ray of light is blocked by the vertical polarizing filter, it cannot be reflected by the mirror, and part of the display will therefore look black. The microprocessor controls which areas of the display appear dark or light, causing them to form numbers. Here it has formed the number 2.

Electronic timekeeper

The base of the watch contains the timekeeping crystal and an electronic microprocessor or "chip." Electricity from the battery makes the crystal vibrate, and the chip counts the number of vibrations to tell how much time has passed. The chip then produces electric signals that control the liquid crystal, thereby causing the watch to display the correct time in minutes and seconds.

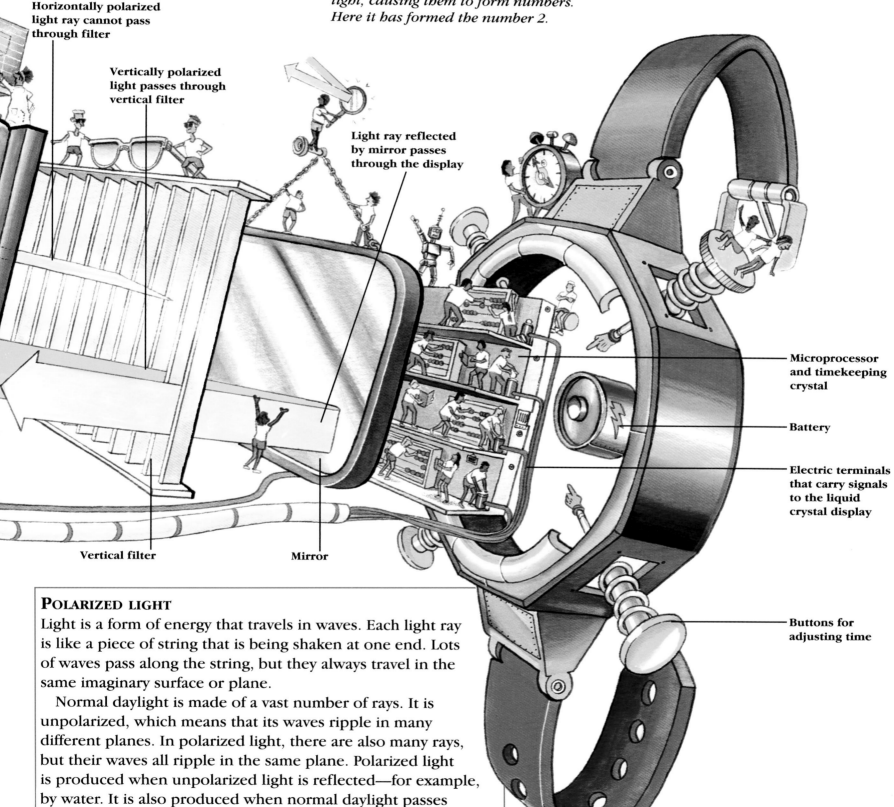

Horizontally polarized light ray cannot pass through filter

Vertically polarized light passes through vertical filter

Light ray reflected by mirror passes through the display

Vertical filter

Mirror

Microprocessor and timekeeping crystal

Battery

Electric terminals that carry signals to the liquid crystal display

Buttons for adjusting time

POLARIZED LIGHT

Light is a form of energy that travels in waves. Each light ray is like a piece of string that is being shaken at one end. Lots of waves pass along the string, but they always travel in the same imaginary surface or plane.

Normal daylight is made of a vast number of rays. It is unpolarized, which means that its waves ripple in many different planes. In polarized light, there are also many rays, but their waves all ripple in the same plane. Polarized light is produced when unpolarized light is reflected—for example, by water. It is also produced when normal daylight passes through special filters, such as the ones used in polarizing sunglasses or the liquid crystal display of a digital watch.

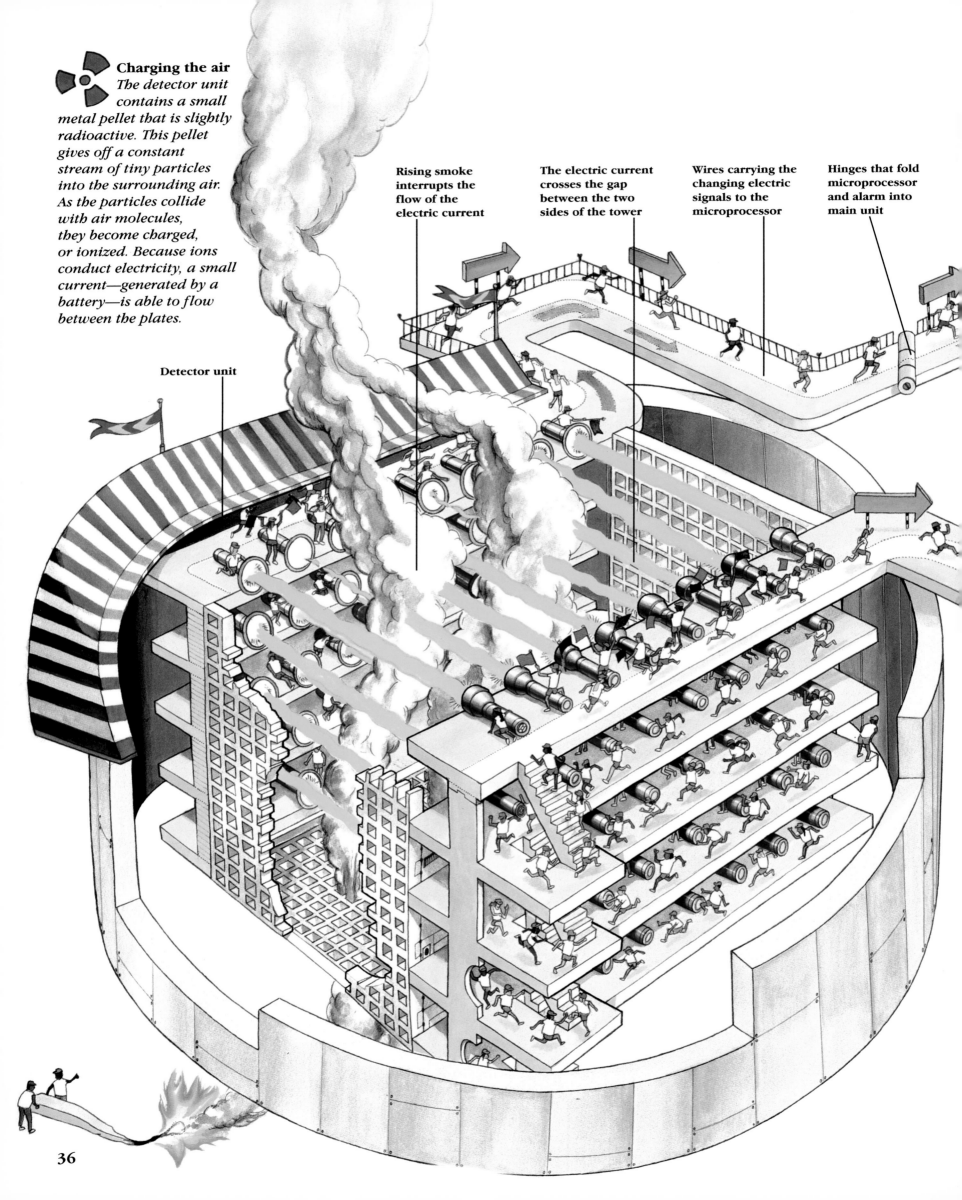

Charging the air
The detector unit contains a small metal pellet that is slightly radioactive. This pellet gives off a constant stream of tiny particles into the surrounding air. As the particles collide with air molecules, they become charged, or ionized. Because ions conduct electricity, a small current—generated by a battery—is able to flow between the plates.

Detector unit

Rising smoke interrupts the flow of the electric current

The electric current crosses the gap between the two sides of the tower

Wires carrying the changing electric signals to the microprocessor

Hinges that fold microprocessor and alarm into main unit

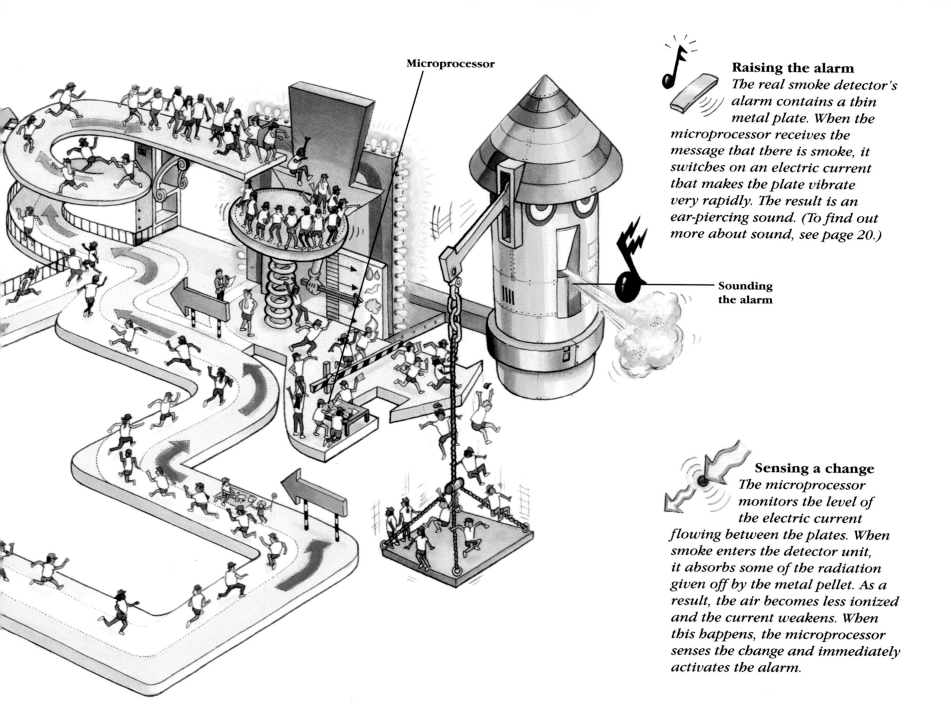

Microprocessor

Raising the alarm
The real smoke detector's alarm contains a thin metal plate. When the microprocessor receives the message that there is smoke, it switches on an electric current that makes the plate vibrate very rapidly. The result is an ear-piercing sound. (To find out more about sound, see page 20.)

Sounding the alarm

Sensing a change
The microprocessor monitors the level of the electric current flowing between the plates. When smoke enters the detector unit, it absorbs some of the radiation given off by the metal pellet. As a result, the air becomes less ionized and the current weakens. When this happens, the microprocessor senses the change and immediately activates the alarm.

Detector unit
The detector unit consists of two metal plates, placed about one inch (2.5 cm) apart, that are connected to a battery. In this detector, the plates are represented by the two opposite sides of a five-story tower.

Normally, it would be very difficult to cross the gap between the plates. But in the real smoke detector, the air between the plates is ionized, or electrically charged, by a stream of weak radiation. This makes it possible for a small current to flow between the plates. The current is represented here by the light rays crossing the gap between the two sides of the tower.

As long as the current flow remains steady, the detector will stay silent. But should smoke spread between the plates, the current will be disrupted, and the alarm will be triggered.

Smoke Alarm

Just as there is no smoke without fire, there is rarely a fire without smoke. Because smoke spreads very quickly, it is often the first sign that a fire has broken out.

The human nose is sensitive and is quite good at smelling smoke. But it does not work well if you are asleep or when you have a cold. Also, it can only smell what is in your immediate surroundings, so it is not much help if your door is firmly shut and a fire starts in another room. This is where a smoke detector comes in handy. As soon as it senses smoke, an alarm is triggered that rings loudly throughout the house.

Videocassette Recorder

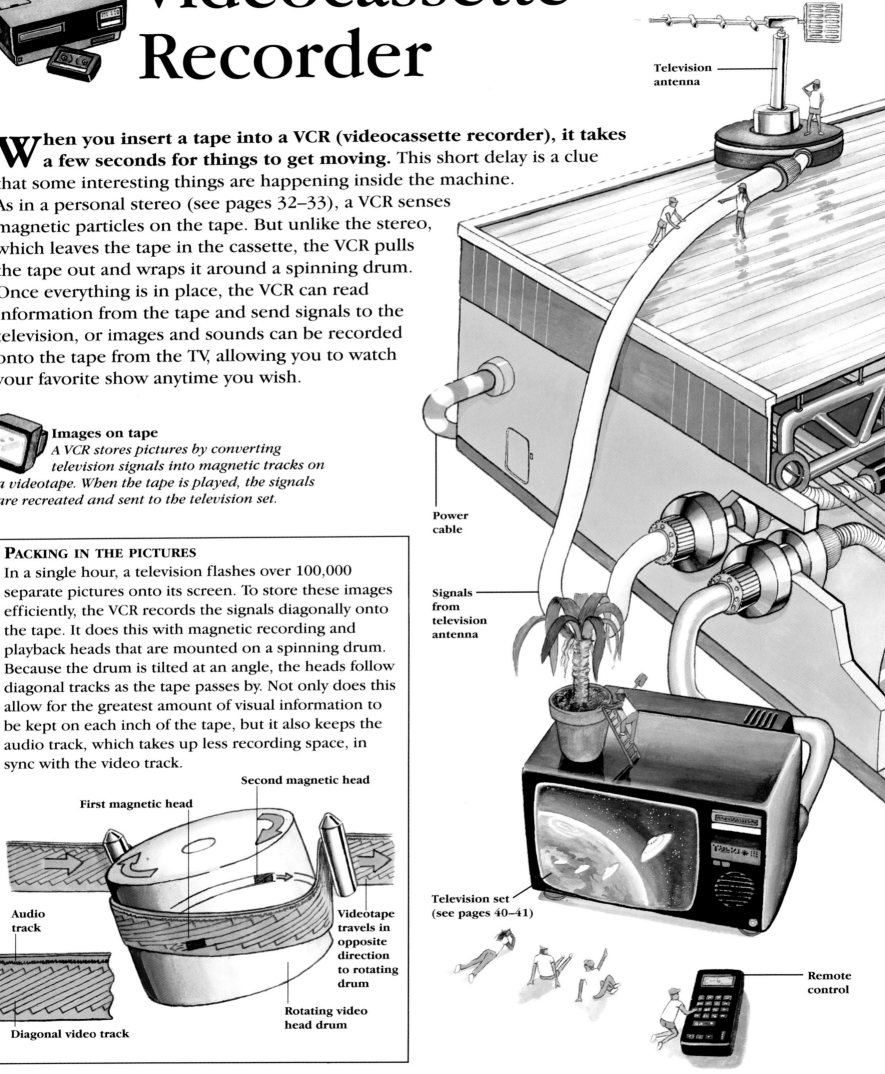

When you insert a tape into a VCR (videocassette recorder), it takes a few seconds for things to get moving. This short delay is a clue that some interesting things are happening inside the machine. As in a personal stereo (see pages 32–33), a VCR senses magnetic particles on the tape. But unlike the stereo, which leaves the tape in the cassette, the VCR pulls the tape out and wraps it around a spinning drum. Once everything is in place, the VCR can read information from the tape and send signals to the television, or images and sounds can be recorded onto the tape from the TV, allowing you to watch your favorite show anytime you wish.

Images on tape
A VCR stores pictures by converting television signals into magnetic tracks on a videotape. When the tape is played, the signals are recreated and sent to the television set.

Television antenna

Power cable

Signals from television antenna

Television set (see pages 40–41)

Remote control

PACKING IN THE PICTURES
In a single hour, a television flashes over 100,000 separate pictures onto its screen. To store these images efficiently, the VCR records the signals diagonally onto the tape. It does this with magnetic recording and playback heads that are mounted on a spinning drum. Because the drum is tilted at an angle, the heads follow diagonal tracks as the tape passes by. Not only does this allow for the greatest amount of visual information to be kept on each inch of the tape, but it also keeps the audio track, which takes up less recording space, in sync with the video track.

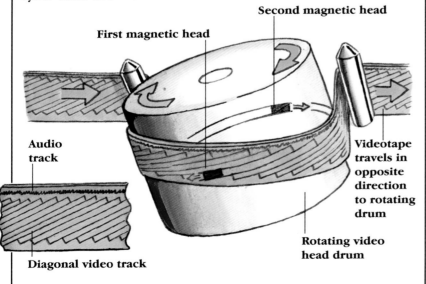

First magnetic head

Second magnetic head

Audio track

Videotape travels in opposite direction to rotating drum

Rotating video head drum

Diagonal video track

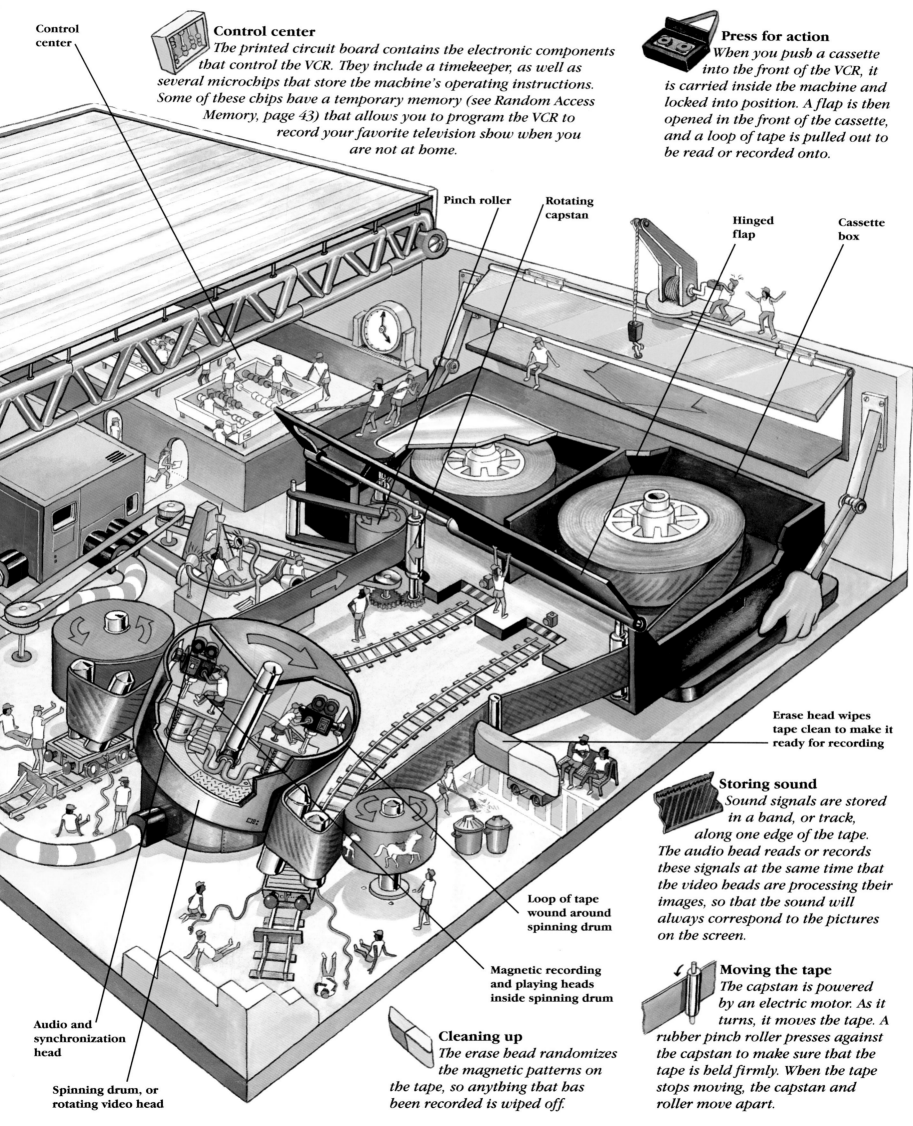

Control center

Control center
The printed circuit board contains the electronic components that control the VCR. They include a timekeeper, as well as several microchips that store the machine's operating instructions. Some of these chips have a temporary memory (see Random Access Memory, page 43) that allows you to program the VCR to record your favorite television show when you are not at home.

Press for action
When you push a cassette into the front of the VCR, it is carried inside the machine and locked into position. A flap is then opened in the front of the cassette, and a loop of tape is pulled out to be read or recorded onto.

Pinch roller

Rotating capstan

Hinged flap

Cassette box

Erase head wipes tape clean to make it ready for recording

Storing sound
Sound signals are stored in a band, or track, along one edge of the tape. The audio head reads or records these signals at the same time that the video heads are processing their images, so that the sound will always correspond to the pictures on the screen.

Loop of tape wound around spinning drum

Magnetic recording and playing heads inside spinning drum

Audio and synchronization head

Cleaning up
The erase head randomizes the magnetic patterns on the tape, so anything that has been recorded is wiped off.

Moving the tape
The capstan is powered by an electric motor. As it turns, it moves the tape. A rubber pinch roller presses against the capstan to make sure that the tape is held firmly. When the tape stops moving, the capstan and roller move apart.

Spinning drum, or rotating video head

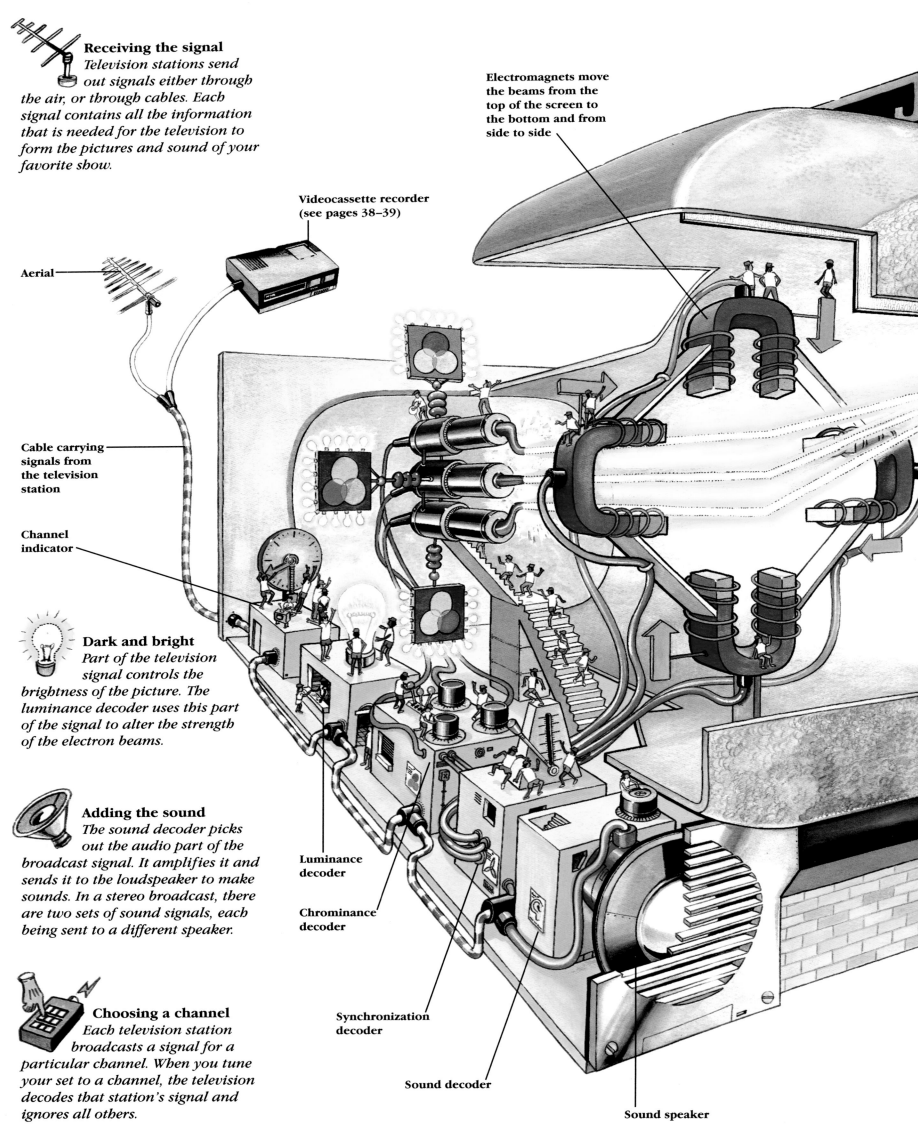

Receiving the signal
Television stations send out signals either through the air, or through cables. Each signal contains all the information that is needed for the television to form the pictures and sound of your favorite show.

Electromagnets move the beams from the top of the screen to the bottom and from side to side

Videocassette recorder (see pages 38–39)

Aerial

Cable carrying signals from the television station

Channel indicator

Dark and bright
Part of the television signal controls the brightness of the picture. The luminance decoder uses this part of the signal to alter the strength of the electron beams.

Adding the sound
The sound decoder picks out the audio part of the broadcast signal. It amplifies it and sends it to the loudspeaker to make sounds. In a stereo broadcast, there are two sets of sound signals, each being sent to a different speaker.

Luminance decoder

Chrominance decoder

Choosing a channel
Each television station broadcasts a signal for a particular channel. When you tune your set to a channel, the television decodes that station's signal and ignores all others.

Synchronization decoder

Sound decoder

Sound speaker

40

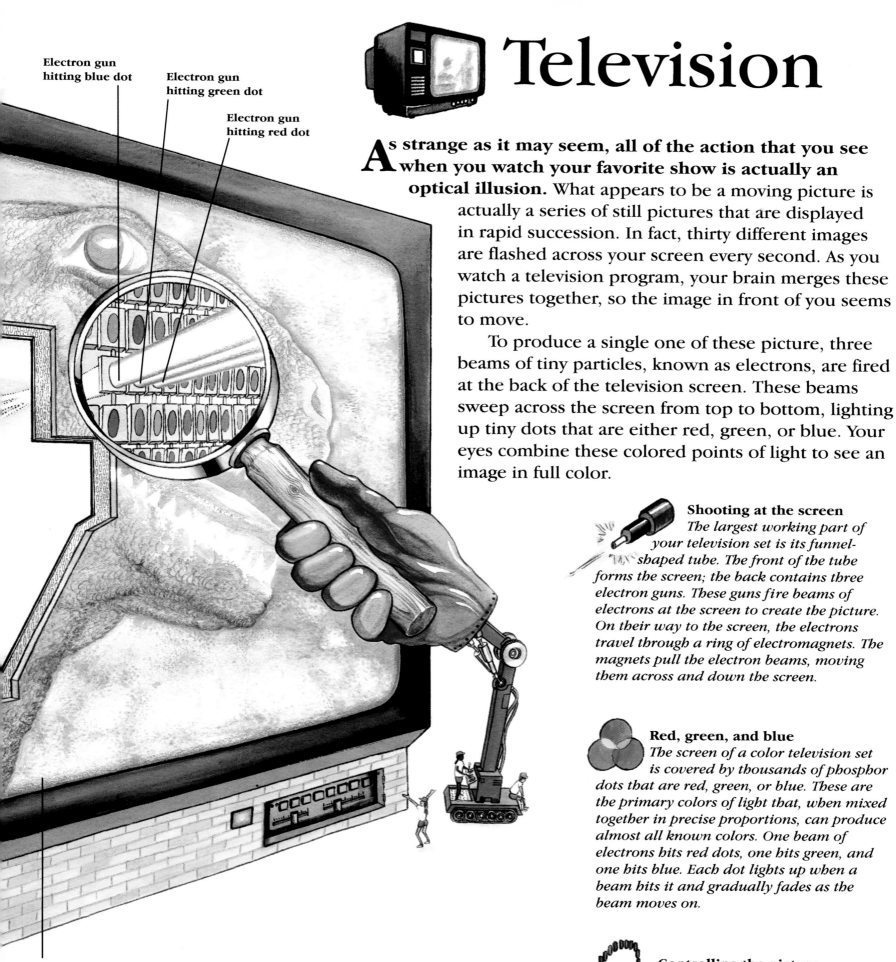

Electron gun
hitting blue dot

Electron gun
hitting green dot

Electron gun
hitting red dot

Television

As strange as it may seem, all of the action that you see when you watch your favorite show is actually an optical illusion. What appears to be a moving picture is actually a series of still pictures that are displayed in rapid succession. In fact, thirty different images are flashed across your screen every second. As you watch a television program, your brain merges these pictures together, so the image in front of you seems to move.

To produce a single one of these picture, three beams of tiny particles, known as electrons, are fired at the back of the television screen. These beams sweep across the screen from top to bottom, lighting up tiny dots that are either red, green, or blue. Your eyes combine these colored points of light to see an image in full color.

Shooting at the screen
The largest working part of your television set is its funnel-shaped tube. The front of the tube forms the screen; the back contains three electron guns. These guns fire beams of electrons at the screen to create the picture. On their way to the screen, the electrons travel through a ring of electromagnets. The magnets pull the electron beams, moving them across and down the screen.

Red, green, and blue
The screen of a color television set is covered by thousands of phosphor dots that are red, green, or blue. These are the primary colors of light that, when mixed together in precise proportions, can produce almost all known colors. One beam of electrons hits red dots, one hits green, and one hits blue. Each dot lights up when a beam hits it and gradually fades as the beam moves on.

The screen is made
of thousands of
red, blue, and
green dots

Moving the beams
The synchronization decoder must identify the part of the signal that acts like a clock to make the electron beams travel across and down the screen at exactly the right speed. In this manner, thirty separate images are flashed across the television screen each and every second.

Controlling the picture
The main part of the television signal is used to control which colored dots will be lit at any given moment. The chrominance decoder identifies this part of the signal and uses it to trigger each of the electron beams at exactly the right instant. If all of the beams were to be triggered continuously, the screen would simply look white. But with this decoder, the television can create a detailed image on the screen.

Computer

Although you may not realize it, computers have an enormous impact on our everyday lives. From supermarket checkouts and offices to cars and jumbo jets, computers are constantly being used to aid us in our daily endeavors.

Computers work by turning information into a stream of electrical pulses. The electrical pulses in this computer are represented by the people working inside it. Just as in a real computer, programs (detailed sets of instructions) are being carried out and calculations are performed with unbelievable speed.

The hard drive
The hard drive is used to store information, including programs and data files. When activated, a disk inside the hard drive spins at high speed. A special arm moves across it and magnetically reads information from the disk, records new information onto it, or erases unwanted files. A program is able to run only after it has been loaded from the hard drive into the RAM (Random-Access Memory).

What's a chip?
A microchip contains thousands or millions of electronic switches, all packed into an extremely small space. By using pulses of electricity, the switches can be turned on or off with lightning speed. Each switch represents one unit of information, called a bit. A powerful chip can store and process millions of bits a second. A collection of bits can represent anything from words or music to complex 3-D images.

Floppy disks
A floppy disk works in the same way as the spinning disk in the hard drive, although it cannot store as much information. A floppy disk can also be used to transfer information from one computer to another.

Signals on the move
Inside the computer, the different microchips are connected by printed circuits. Electric signals flash along these circuits almost instantaneously, enabling the computer to process information very quickly.

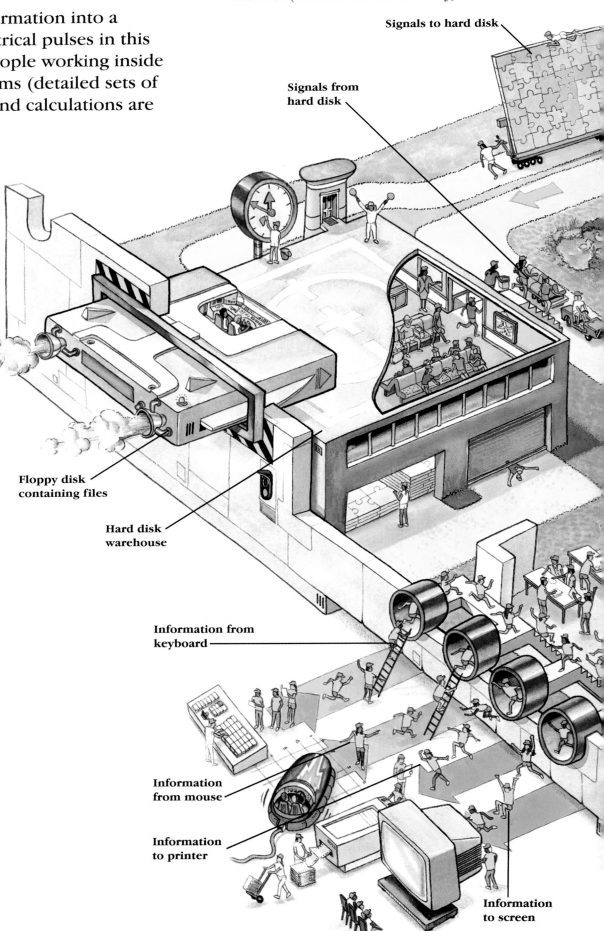

Signals to hard disk

Signals from hard disk

Floppy disk containing files

Hard disk warehouse

Information from keyboard

Information from mouse

Information to printer

Information to screen

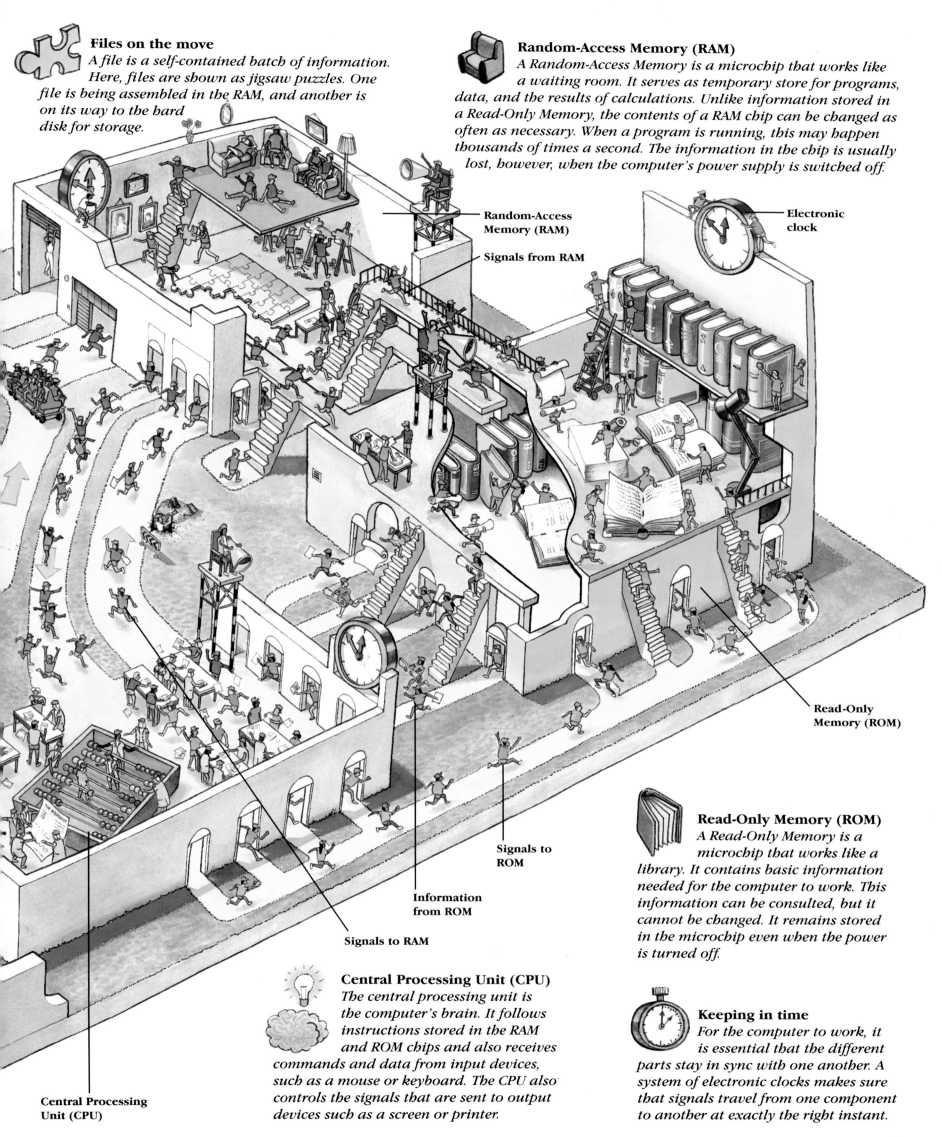

Files on the move
A file is a self-contained batch of information. Here, files are shown as jigsaw puzzles. One file is being assembled in the RAM, and another is on its way to the hard disk for storage.

Random-Access Memory (RAM)
A Random-Access Memory is a microchip that works like a waiting room. It serves as temporary store for programs, data, and the results of calculations. Unlike information stored in a Read-Only Memory, the contents of a RAM chip can be changed as often as necessary. When a program is running, this may happen thousands of times a second. The information in the chip is usually lost, however, when the computer's power supply is switched off.

Random-Access Memory (RAM)

Signals from RAM

Electronic clock

Read-Only Memory (ROM)

Signals to ROM

Information from ROM

Signals to RAM

Central Processing Unit (CPU)

Read-Only Memory (ROM)
A Read-Only Memory is a microchip that works like a library. It contains basic information needed for the computer to work. This information can be consulted, but it cannot be changed. It remains stored in the microchip even when the power is turned off.

Central Processing Unit (CPU)
The central processing unit is the computer's brain. It follows instructions stored in the RAM and ROM chips and also receives commands and data from input devices, such as a mouse or keyboard. The CPU also controls the signals that are sent to output devices such as a screen or printer.

Keeping in time
For the computer to work, it is essential that the different parts stay in sync with one another. A system of electronic clocks makes sure that signals travel from one component to another at exactly the right instant.

43

Glossary

amplify
To make something larger or greater. An amplifier works by strengthening an electrical current.

aperture
In a camera, the opening that lets light shine onto the film. The wider the aperture, the more light that is allowed in.

atom
The smallest complete particle of a solid, liquid, or gas. Atoms make up everything, from the air we breathe to the machines we use.

attract
To pull or draw something without actually touching it. A magnet attracts some kinds of metal.

axle
A rotating rod. Axles turn wheels, or transfer movement from one place to another.

battery
A device that stores energy. Batteries contain chemical energy that can be turned into electrical energy.

bearing
Parts of a machine, such as ball bearings, that reduce friction. Bearings separate moving surfaces, allowing one surface to slide easily past another.

bimetallic strip
A strip made of two different kinds of metal bonded together. Because the two metals react differently to heat, they expand at different rates,

pulling away from one another and causing the whole strip to bend.

cam
A device that changes rotary movement into linear movement. It is shaped like a lopsided wheel.

carbon
An element that is most often found in coal. Pure forms of carbon are graphite and diamond. Carbon particles are used in some devices to help conduct electricity.

chrominance
In a television signal, the information that regulates colors on the screen.

circuit
The complete path of an electric current. Electrical circuits include the energy source and can be many miles long.

compressor
A device that squeezes a liquid or a gas, forcing it into a smaller space.

condense
To turn from a gas or vapor into a liquid. Gases and vapors condense either when they are cooled or when they are compressed.

decoder
A device that unscrambles messages into a form that can be understood. In a television set, it turns transmission signals into pictures and sound.

diaphragm
A thin, flexible disk that vibrates. Diaphragms can generate sound waves and can also convert them into electricity.

electrical contact
The meeting point of two electrical conductors through which

electricity flows. Most electrical contacts are made of metal.

electric current
A flow of charged particles, called electrons, which carry energy. When an electric current is turned on, electricity can travel miles in an instant.

electromagnet
A magnet surrounded by a coil through which electricity flows. The electric current, rather than the metal bar, causes the magnetism.

electron
A tiny particle that conisists of a negative electric charge. Electrons that flow together make up an electric current. All atoms contain electrons.

electron beam
A stream of electrons that move through air or empty space. In a television, the energy from electron beams is converted into light to make a picture.

electronic
Something that uses small pulses of electricity to operate.

emit
To give off something. For example, a light bulb emits light, an oven emits heat.

enzyme
A substance that greatly speeds up a chemical reaction.

evaporate
To turn a liquid into a vapor (a gaseous state). Water evaporates slowly if it is left in a dry place.

fluctuate
To vary, or shift back and forth.

friction
A force that slows down motion

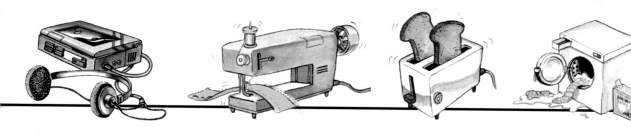

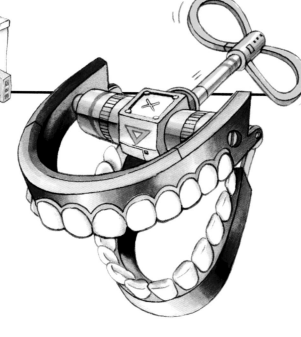

between two or more objects that are in contact with one another. Friction can be reduced by use of oil or bearings, but it can never be completely eliminated.

gear
A toothed wheel that is designed to transfer movement in a machine. Gears can change a movement's speed, force, or direction.

heat-resistant
Something that is not easily damaged by heat and that slows down the movement of heat from one material to another.

hinge
A jointed device on which a door or other moving part turns.

impulse
In electronics, a short burst of electricity. Electrical impulses can be used to carry information.

insulate
To block the path of heat, sound, or electricity. Plastics, glass, ceramics, and rubber are insulating materials.

interact
To have an effect on something while at the same time being affected by it.

ionized
Made entirely or partly of ions. Ions are atoms that have gained or lost at least one electron and have a positive or negative charge.

luminance
The amount and intensity of light on a surface. In a television signal, it is the information that controls the brightness or dimness of the picture.

magnetic field
The space around a magnet or

current in which forces can be detected. The field is strongest in the area closest to the body producing the pull or current.

magnetism
The pulling force that attracts certain metals and is produced by a magnet. Magnetism can be permanent, or, in the case of an electromagnet, it can be switched on and off.

microprocessor
An electronic device that carries out calculations. Microprocessors are at the heart of most computers and calculators.

molecule
The smallest particle of any given substance that still retains all the properties of that substance. A molecule is composed of one or more atoms.

monitor
To keep something under constant watch or surveillance.

nozzle
A narrow opening at the end of a pipe or tube that speeds up or directs the flow of fluid or gas.

phosphor
A substance that glows or emits light when struck by an electron beam or radiation.

plane
A completely flat surface.

pressure
The force that things exert upon their surroundings. The pressure of a gas or vapor in a container will increase if heated.

prism
A transparent object with flat sides used to refract or disperse light. The most common type is wedge-shaped.

program
In computing, a list of instructions that a computer follows. Although the instructions may be simple, there are often very many of them.

radiation
Energy emitted in the form of waves or particles. Light and radiowaves are both forms of radiation.

radioactive
Something that gives off energy in the form of radiation. Some radioactive substances are dangerous because their radiation harms living things.

random
Having no definite order or pattern.

repel
To push something away without actually touching it. Magnets repel each other if their matching poles are near one another.

sound waves
Waves of pressure that we interpret as sound.

valve
A device that permits liquid or gas to flow through a passage in one direction only.

vapor
A gas that forms as a result of the evaporation of a liquid.

Index